S0-ABD-596

WITHDRAWN
FROM THE
COLLECTION

Oakland Public Library
Oakland, CA
www.oaklandlibrary.org

Disasters

NOV 2 3 2005

DISASTERS

Wasted Lives, Valuable Lessons

Randall Bell

with

Donald T. Phillips

Tapestry Press
Irving, Texas

Tapestry Press
3649 Conflans Road
Suite 103
Irving, TX 75061

Copyright © 2005 by Randall Bell

All Rights Reserved
No part of this work may be reproduced or transmitted in any form or
by any means, electrical or mechanical, including photocopying, or
by any information storage or retrieval system, without the written
permission of the author.

Printed in the U.S.A.
09 08 07 06 05 1 2 3 4 5

Library of Congress Cataloging-in-Publication Data
Bell, Randall.
  Disasters : wasted lives, valuable lessons / by Randall Bell with Donald T.
Phillips.
     p. cm.
  Summary: "Documents the details and the aftermath in financial and human
terms of ten of the world's most tragic events"--Provided by publisher.
  Includes bibliographical references and index.
  ISBN 1-930819-43-9 (trade paper : alk. paper)
  1. Disasters--Case studies. 2. Disasters--Economic aspects. 3. Real prop-
erty--Valuation. 4. Emergency management. I. Phillips, Donald T. (Donald
Thomas), 1952- II. Title.
  HV553.B46 2005
  363.34--dc22
                                        2005005829

Photo on lower left of front cover is White House photo by Paul Morse.
Photos in this book with no credit attached are either in the public domain or it
was not possible to determine the source of the photographs after extensive
research and it is believed that they are in the public domain.

Page design and layout by
D. & F. Scott Publishing, Inc.
N. Richland Hills, Texas

Contents

Introduction

The entire world gasped over the devastating effects of the December 2004 Asian tsunami off the coast of Sumatra in the Indian Ocean. As do all tsunamis, this disaster started with an earthquake. The fourth largest since 1900, its 9.0 magnitude on the Richter Scale released energy equivalent to 23,000 Hiroshima-sized atomic bombs. Huge ocean waves were generated heading out in all directions from the earthquake's epicenter. Traveling at up to 500 miles per hour (as fast as a commercial jet liner), when they finally reached the shores of Indonesia, some measured up to 33 feet in height. Unprecedented damages occurred in thirteen countries, including: Indonesia, Sri Lanka, India, Thailand, Myanmar, Malaysia, The Maldives, and Somalia. More than 300,000 people were killed, 500,000 injured, and 5 million left homeless. The estimated cost of reconstruction was $7.5 billion—and the total international aid promised to the tsunami-ravaged nations was in excess of $7 billion.

In the Asian tsunami's aftermath, an obvious question arose: What will change as a result of this natural disaster? From prior experience, we already know that there are four likely outcomes:

➤ 1. High-risk tsunami districts will be established throughout the Indian Ocean.

➤ 2. "Blow-out" designs will be established for new and rebuilt resorts—where lower floors are used for parking and walls are designed to "blow out" so that water may pass through the structure.

➤ 3. Vertical evacuation systems will be put in place—where helicopter pads are placed on building roofs and signs are put up warning people to move upward rather than down to the street.

➤ 4. A new "buoy-based" tsunami warning system will be established throughout the Indian Ocean.

Just how do we know these four changes will be implemented in the wake of the Asian tsunami? Because that is exactly what happened in the aftermath of the three major Hawaiian tsunami disasters of the twentieth century (1946, 1952, and 1960).

A tsunami wave approaches shore.

Banda Aceh, Sumatra, Indonesia, Jan. 14, 2005.

U.S. Navy photo by Petty Officer 3rd Class Tyler J. Clements

And therein lies one of the major points of this book.

It is very rare to ever come across a disaster (natural or man made) that has not previously occurred, has not been thoroughly studied, and has not had its impacts and lessons analyzed. Of course, most people look at these disasters and learn from them. However, a significant number ignore the lessons learned and move forward with an "it-can't-happen-to- me-attitude."

In the following pages, ten of the world's most famous disasters are analyzed. We discuss the disaster itself, what the disaster site looks like today, the impact on real estate values, and some of the wide-ranging lessons learned. By studying these disasters, as painful as that can sometimes be, we can minimize the impact of similar future disasters and, in the cases of some of those that are man made, actually prevent them from ever happening again.

A village near the coast of Sumatra lays in ruin.

QuickBird satellite image courtesy of DigitalGlobe

QuickBird satellite image courtesy of DigitalGlobe

Satellite imagery showing the northern shore of Banda Aceh six months before the tsunami (top) and on December 28, 2004, two days after the tsunami (below).

1

Chernobyl Nuclear Meltdown

Chernobyl, Ukraine [Soviet Union]
April 26, 1986

The Disaster

The world's worst nuclear disaster occurred in the obscure village of Chernobyl located along the Prypyat River about eighty miles north of Kiev, Ukraine. It produced an explosion that sent catastrophic clouds of radioactive fallout all across Europe. The resulting radioactive exposure on human life was equivalent to a thousand Hiroshima nuclear bombs.

The Chernobyl nuclear complex, which supplied most of the electricity to Kiev (population 2.5 million) and surrounding areas of the former Soviet Union, consisted of four six-story active reactors manned by five thousand employees. When Reactor #4 was scheduled to be shut down for routine maintenance, some scientists decided to take advantage of the opportunity and conduct an unauthorized experiment. Unfortunately, in setting up the test, they ignored the required approval process and violated key safety rules and regulations.

A nuclear reactor has certain emergency shut off controls in case things get too hot or out of balance. But the scientists turned off those controls because they planned to power-down the reactor so low that an emergency shut off would not be necessary. Basically, they wanted to see how much electrical power would be stored in the event of a shutdown—and if there would be enough power left to operate the emergency equipment and core cooling pumps. The scientists, however, did not completely think through this very dangerous procedure. Nor did they respect the fact that they were dealing with enormous quantities of refined uranium that produce extraordinarily high levels of radioactivity.

During the procedure, the power of the Reactor #4 was gradually cut to 10 percent of capacity. Then the steam lines that surround the core were switched off. These lines were heated by rods of uranium centered in a geometric array in the core of reactor. The heat from those steam lines ultimately spun a generator that, in turn, produced the massive electrical power supplied to customers. But with the steam lines cut off, the reactor itself began to overheat—and the power fell to such an alarmingly low level that the entire reactor became unstable. In an effort to cool the system and increase the power, the scientists withdrew most of the uranium rods. At first, this move appeared to solve the problem. But when the uranium rods were reinserted, there was a sudden rise in temperature and an enormous surge of power.

Photo by Randall Bell

The Chernobyl nuclear power plant.

At 1:23 AM, the reactor core exploded in a mammoth fireball. The explosion blew off the reactor's heavy steel and concrete lid killing thirty-one people and injuring many more. Fifty tons of radioactive atomic fuel vented into the atmosphere while an additional seventy tons burned through the twelve-foot concrete slab and melted into the ground. The air became thick with smoke and dust. Near the core, the radiation became so intense that it destroyed people's central nervous systems and killed them in minutes. Farther away, both adults and children became covered with a milky white dust and felt a prickly feeling in their throats.

From a distance, it appeared only as though the nuclear reactor was on fire. And initially, the Soviet authorities told their citizens that there had been a slight mishap and the building's roof was on fire. The community was oblivious to the fact that there had been a nuclear catastrophe and that the smoke, fumes, and dust pouring from the ensuing fire were highly radioactive and extremely dangerous.

As firemen were sent in the facility to get the fire under control, local residents came out to view the scene. Hundreds of local school children were also

Closeup of damage to the Chernobyl plant.

taken to a bridge overlooking the site so they could admire the brave firefighters.

For the first day and a half, Soviet authorities kept quiet as to the reality of the situation. They brought in helicopters that dumped bags of wet sand, lead, and boron graphite onto the reactor. They sent welders and miners into the core to dig under the reactor and pump liquid nitrogen in to cool the reactor. All this was done in an effort to get the blaze and the venting of radiation under control.

Meanwhile, there were gigantic plumes of highly radioactive material rising into the sky and fanning out over Northern Europe. These clouds drifted across the Prypyat River and floated through the city of Prypyat (40,000 population), through Kiev (population 2.5 million), over the entire state of Belarus, continued on up to Sweden, and floated as far west as Scotland and Ireland where the radioactive material settled into grasses where sheep were grazing.

Entrance to the Chernobyl exclusion zone.

Photo by Randall Bell

Swedish scientists were the first to detect high levels of radiation in the air. They determined the source was emanating from somewhere inside the Soviet Union and began to demand answers. The Soviets initially denied there was a problem. But when alarms sounded at one of Scotland's nuclear power plants, the international community began to think something sinister was going on. Are the Soviets trying to kill us, people wondered? Are they doing this intentionally? What is happening?

Finally, under tremendous political pressure, the Soviet ambassador in London publicly acknowledged the disaster. The news made headlines all over the world. Soviet President Mikhail Gorbachev subsequently addressed his nation. "Good evening, comrades," he said. "All of you know that there has been an incredible misfortune—the accident at the Chernobyl nuclear plant. It has painfully affected the Soviet people, and shocked the international community. For the first time, we confront the real force of nuclear energy, out of control."

The village of Chernobyl and the city of Prypyat were subsequently evacuated in a matter of hours. More than 135,000 people within twenty miles of the reactor were also forced to leave their homes as fast as humanly possible. Radioactive levels in Kiev (the third largest city in the Soviet Union) were measured at 300 times the maximum safe level. In something of a mass panic, one million people evacuated the city—some so desperate to leave that they threw themselves on the roofs of departing trains. And hundreds of thousands of Ukrainians, Russians, and Belorussians abandoned entire cities and settlements in the path of the radioactive cloud.

After the Soviet leaders finally "fessed up," people and money from all over the world poured into Chernobyl. A twenty-story "sarcophagus" was hastily constructed—paid for by international funds because the Soviets didn't have the cash on hand to finance the operation. The Chernobyl nuclear meltdown, itself, lasted for ten days before finally being contained. In the following days, weeks, and months, more than 600,000 people were involved in a cleanup that cost an estimated $60 billion.

The disaster at Chernobyl had catastrophic and long-lasting repercussions. Hundreds of thousands of people had to be resettled. An estimated twenty million were exposed to high levels of radiation—resulting in numerous health consequences, including: birth defects, leukemia, and unusually high levels of thyroid cancer. Ultimately, the meltdown may be responsible for causing 300,000 total deaths.

The resulting economic impact on the USSR was also catastrophic. The Soviets were exposed as being both inept and insolvent. Five years after Chernobyl, the Soviet Union split apart and, along with it, the communist block in Eastern Europe.

The Disaster Site Today

My visit to the Chernobyl disaster site took considerable time and effort. Jut to get in the general vicinity I had to fly to Kiev, the capital city of Ukraine. Then I found a local entrepreneur who was willing to rent me his car for the day and I began the two-hour journey north. It's a pleasant drive with long stretches of green countryside and numerous small villages along the way. Well into the drive, I was thinking to myself about how remote and pleasant a place Chernobyl must be when I came upon a high security checkpoint loaded with countless World War II-type land barricades and manned by several machinegun-toting military guards. This, I quickly learned, was edge of the seventeen-mile exclusion zone that surrounds the nuclear disaster site.

Brandishing my letter of invitation from the mayor of Chernobyl, I expected to be admitted without delay and possibly escorted along the final part of my journey. But that's not the way it worked out. I was questioned extensively about who I was, what I was doing there, and what I wanted to accomplish. After hours of talks, I was finally taken into a room where I underwent a full-body atomic detection scan (which would also be done when I left the exclusion zone). The Ukrainian guards eventually warmed up and offered me a nice lunch that included traditional Russian vodka. Somehow I felt that vodka and machine guns were not a good mix, but the guards turned out to be terrific guys with a great sense of humor.

Feeling more comfortable, I hopped back in my car and drove toward the nuclear power plant. The next fifteen miles or so was, I felt, unusually quiet. There were not many people around and no birds that I could see. Soon, I came upon another guard shack that protected a 1.5-mile exclusion zone around the epicenter of the disaster. Beyond were the communities of Chernobyl and Prypyat. This exclusion zone is so hot (radioactivitywise) that very few visitors are allowed through—and no material indigenous to the environment is allowed out. My paperwork was in order so I was admitted without delay.

Within minutes, I was driving through the small village of Chernobyl. It was not unlike the other communities I had driven through on the trip from Kiev. But there was one major difference. There were no people around. It was totally deserted. When I got to the nuclear power plant, I was astonished to learn that it was still operational. I drove past two partially completed reactor buildings that had been under construction at the time of the disaster. Still there was a huge abandoned crane hovering over the construction sites. At the first of the three operational reactors, I met my guide, a woman named Inna who spoke fluent English although she had never been to an English-speaking country.

Inna hopped in the car with me and we drove to Reactor #4, site of the world's worst nuclear disaster. A vast gray sarcophagus enclosed the original six-story structure. I was surprised at how huge it was—I mean, it was really immense. We pulled up to the entrance and got out of the car. Inna informed me that it was safe to go into the reactor for ten minutes if I wished. But she was going to stay outside. I already knew that the concrete tomb had accumulated forty tons of radioactive dust inside, so I politely said, "No, thanks." Besides, I was more interested in seeing the impact this event had on surrounding areas.

Next to Reactor #4 there were some pretty dense forests and, as we walked around, I was surprised by the abundant wildlife. I saw wild boars, deer, and a lynx. The foliage was lush and green. But upon closer inspection, I noticed some strange growth patterns. The pine trees, for instance, which usually grow in groups of three needles to a stem of uniform length, had two and four needles to a stem—some of various lengths and wandering in random directions. They had lost what scientists call "spatial relationships."

After a while, we got back in the car and drove across the river and into Prypyat. This was a fairly large city (much larger than Chernobyl) but it was completely deserted—a real ghost town. We turned one corner and saw old carnival rides such as Ferris wheels, bumper cars, etc.—all of which were covered with radioactive gray dust. Inna informed me that the accident had occurred a week before May Day—a holiday of major significance in Eastern Europe—and the city was preparing for a large celebration.

After crossing the river, we stopped the car and walked around. We went into the Soviet nuclear offices and into some the hotels and shops. It was very eerie walking around and seeing no people, no cars, and absolutely no movement. We walked all over the place for the next several hours. And at every location, there was a steady clicking of the Geiger counter Inna was carrying. She was constantly monitoring radioactivity intensities to make sure we didn't get into too hot an area. At one point, I put one of my cameras on the ground, but she quickly scolded me and told to never, ever put anything on the highly radioactive ground. I did not make that mistake again.

At one point, we hiked across some overgrown grassy areas and entered a deserted elementary school. The sight was something I'll never forget. There were colorful cartoon murals everywhere. And there were desks, chairs, toys, dolls, cribs, and a couple of pianos—all covered with that same gray radioactive dust. The kids had their names written on a bulletin board for that day's assignments. I stepped over a pair of white shoes that looked just like a pair my own three-year-old daughter wore back home. In this setting, it did not take a lot of imagination to envision the children impacted by this terrible disaster.

In one of the classrooms, there was a large poster with cartoon characters that described what the children should do if and when the Americans dropped nuclear bombs on the Soviet Union. On a wood shelf, there were bottles of unused Potassium Iodine pills to take for radiation sickness after the bombs exploded. I looked out a window of that same classroom and could see a large missile defense system designed to protect the city from such an attack. A quick reading of our Geiger counter revealed that our radioactive exposure was now three to four times the maximum safe level.

Photo by Randall Bell

The elementary school in the village of Chernobyl.

Inside a classroom of the elementary school at Chernobyl. The entire class-room is covered with radioactive fallout.

We soon left the school and walked on a path the children and their teachers took to the bridge separating Prypyat from Chernobyl. Then we stood on that same bridge where the kids admired the efforts of the brave firefighters who were working hard to put out the flames. There was a light breeze blowing in our faces—and I could imagine how the children had inhaled the highly radioactive dust, smoke, and fumes. Many of these children developed deep scars on their necks from the negative effects of thyroid cancer. Doctors refer to the scars as a "nuclear necklace." Most of these children died of thyroid cancer brought on by the exposure from radiation—not from the fallout of a U. S. nuclear explosion, as feared—but from a nuclear disaster, quite literally, in their own back yard.

Impact and Insight

From a real estate economics perspective, one might expect the property around Chernobyl to have no value whatsoever. Well, of course, it is not a good market. But there really is some value to the real estate.

Let's start with the seventeen-mile exclusion zone. It is mostly open countryside with some large farms and a number of small villages. Officially, nobody is allowed to live in this area. But people do. I saw them and spoke to several of them. They are unofficially termed "resettlers" and are all elderly people who lived in the region prior to the disaster. After being evacuated, many fought to return to the homes where they had lived all their lives. Initially, the Soviet government said no. Upon further reflection, however, they realized that

Cesium 137, the radioactive contaminant released after a nuclear meltdown, takes thirty years to develop cancer in any given individual. There is a very high risk that some form of cancer will develop. But people over sixty years old would most likely die of old age before the cancer got them. So why not let them move back? And that's the way it went.

Today, there are approximately ten thousand people (between the ages of sixty and ninety) living within the seventeen-mile exclusion zone around Chernobyl. Younger family members are allowed to visit once in awhile for brief periods of time. For people under the age of sixty, though, the area is deemed uninhabitable.

Eventually, the land itself could be utilized for some sort of industrial purpose that would involve concrete sites. But estimates range from sixty to two hundred years (depending on where you are in the exclusion zone) before that would be allowed. Farming or any other type of agricultural industry would be dangerous and completely inappropriate for at least two hundred years.

Within the 1.5-mile exclusion zone, there is zero residential real estate value. Nobody is allowed to live there—not in the big city of Prypryat, not in the small village of Chernobyl. There is, however, a value to the industrial real estate for the simple reason that two, sometimes three of the Chernobyl reactors are still operational. Workers are bussed in and out every day at the beginning and end of their shifts. They wear special overalls and high-tech meters that constantly measure their exposure to radiation. And each person undergoes a full body scan every time they enter and leave the facility.

It will be at least two centuries before there is any chance the situation can change within the 1.5-mile exclusion zone. As for the #4 reactor where the meltdown occurred, it will be 20,000 years before the real estate will be fully safe.

Lessons Learned

1. Follow The Rules. They Are There for a Reason

There were specific rules in place at the Chernobyl nuclear facility that, if followed, would have prevented the disaster. But the scientists in charge saw these rules as a barrier to everyday performance and believed they would be better served to ignore them.

In society, we have rules that often may seem like barriers, but things move along much more safely if they are followed. We think of traffic signals, for instance, as hindrances to getting to our destinations quickly. They slow us down. They make us wait. But the reality is that when a stoplight goes out, it backs up traffic or causes accidents. And that makes everybody worse off.

The nuclear scientists at Chernobyl broke the rules and the world suffered dire consequences as a result. The six people primarily responsible for the Chernobyl disaster were sentenced to many years at hard labor in Soviet prisons.

2. In The Aftermath of a Man-Made Disaster, Tell the Truth

Once the top leaders in the Soviet Union knew the full extent of the nuclear meltdown at Chernobyl, they kept quiet, denied there was a problem, and then tried to cover it up. They saw only the short-term benefit of denial and misrepresentation. But events compounded very quickly and, in the long run, the situation was made far worse than if the Soviet leaders had just told the truth from the very beginning.

2

The Love Canal

Niagara Falls, New York
August 7, 1978

The Disaster

At first blush, the "Love" Canal sounds like a romantic place where young couples might ride together in small two-seat boats. In reality, the Love Canal is the mother of all so-called "chemical soup" cases—an outrageous chemical dump that, over the years, became nothing less than a ticking time bomb. Prior to the Love Canal, society was basically working under the belief system that dangerous chemicals and contaminants had a benign effect on the environment and would somehow be absorbed by nature. But this chemical dump—located smack dab in the middle of a populous residential area—changed that false belief system forever. The Love Canal was the very first case study of large-scale environmental contamination.

In 1893, industrialist Colonel William T. Love began construction of what he envisioned to be a ten-mile-long canal that would provide inexpensive electrical power for the future modern industrial city of Niagara Falls. Back in those days, the only type of electricity that had been developed was direct current (DC) where the source had to be close to the user because it did not transmit efficiently over long distances. Col. Love reasoned that the 110-foot drop from the Lake Erie side of the Niagara River to the Lake Ontario side would provide more than enough electrical power to achieve his dream.

Less than a mile of the canal had been completed when a scientist (coincidentally a resident of Niagara Falls) discovered alternating current (AC), which could be transmitted over long distances via power lines. That discovery, for all intents and purposes, made William T. Love's concept obsolete. As a result, his Niagara Power Company went into bankruptcy and construction on the canal ceased when it was only three thousand feet long and one hundred feet wide. Over the ensuing years, the north-south-running canal filled up with rainwater and snow runoff and its sixteen acres were used for recreation where kids swam in the summer and ice-skated in the winter. For more than fifty years, the Love Canal was just a fun place to be. Then along came World War II.

After Pear Harbor was attacked on December 7, 1941, the United States strategically expanded industrial production for the manufacture of war-related materials. Hooker Chemical Company (later Occidental), a heavy industrial manufacturer, was one of hundreds of domestic corporations called upon by the government to increase production. In 1942, Hooker purchased land along the sides of the Love Canal and built large manufacturing facilities along its banks with the express purpose of disposing of chemical wastes directly into the canal. Over the course of the next eleven years (through World War II and the Korean War), Hooker pumped water out of the canal and refilled it with nearly 25,000 tons of toxic chemicals, including acid chlorides, sulfur compounds, TCP, benzyl alcohol, chlorinated hydrocarbon residues, process sludges, fly ash, and other toxic wastes. In addition, the city of Niagara Falls was allowed to dispose of municipal wastes there.

During the timeframe from 1947 to 1952, urban sprawl began to fill the agricultural land surrounding the Love Canal and the Hooker manufacturing facilities. New housing developments (and everything that came with them) were con-

structed. It was no secret that the canal had a lot of bad stuff
buried in it, but the attitudes back then were very cavalier and
people just didn't take it all that seriously. When the manufacturing facilities finally closed in 1953, company engineers, who
were aware that the Love Canal was comprised of a natural clay
bottom, recommended that it also be covered with a clay
"cap." With both an impermeable bottom and top, they reasoned that the chemicals would be efficiently contained.

About this time, the Niagara Falls Board of Education
approached Hooker Chemical with a request to purchase their
property for future development—including the construction
of an elementary school. Initially, the company refused to sell
the land for such a purpose citing the many poisonous chemicals contained in the canal site. But the Board of Education was
very persistent. They placed great pressure on the company's
executives and even alluded to the fact that, if necessary, the
property could be acquired by eminent domain.

The company finally agreed to sell the property with the
stipulation that a deed restriction be inserted that the Canal
site would be maintained as a park and no schools would be

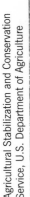

Aerial photos of the Love Canal in 1951 (left) and 1980 (right). The 1980 image
shows the increased surrounding development.

Agricultural Stabilization and Conservation Service, U.S. Department of Agriculture

National Ocean Service, U.S. Department of Commerce

built on it. Ultimately, Hooker transferred the property to the Board of Education for the sum of one dollar. But for a reason that has never been explained, the deed restriction was left out of the sales agreement.

In 1954, the company's warnings were ignored and the 99th Street Public Elementary School was constructed on the old canal site. Also, the city of Niagara Falls constructed roads and sewers through the site—and the state of New York relocated a local street and storm sewer at the southern end of the Love Canal. Then, in 1957, the Board of Education proposed to sell portions of the canal property to private developers for further residential development. But representatives of Hooker Chemical Company showed up at the board's public hearings to protest the idea and repeated their warnings of toxic substances at the site. Hooker also took out advertisements in local newspapers as to the danger of building any residential dwellings on or near the Love Canal. Urban sprawl and residential development, however, did continue in an unabated manner until the area reached full development. Months stretched into years and little was done to monitor the toxicity of the local environment.

By the 1960s, residents began to complain of noxious fumes and chemical substances seeping into basements. In the mid- 1970s, chemical wastes were bubbling to the surface into people's yards and forming puddles on the sidewalks. Children would pick up phosphorous-looking dirt clods and throw them down on the streets to see the

The 99th Street Public Elementary School.

www.onlineethics.org

fiery impacts. The kids called them "fire rocks." There were even reports of fifty-gallon drums popping up into backyards.

After authorities did some testing, it was determined that the clay soils had acted like a giant bathtub to contain rainwater. Over time, that water filled the canal and brought the toxic chemicals to the surface. When it was further discovered that the groundwater table was contaminated, local residents became extremely vocal. Some went all the way to Washington, D.C. with their complaints and the situation soon received high-profile media attention. As a result, on August 7, 1978, the president of the United States declared that a "federal state of emergency" existed for the area. The state of New York followed suit by labeling the Love Canal area "a threat to human health and welfare."

Over the next two years, the federal government purchased at full value the homes closest to the canal and relocated all the residents. The state installed an eight-foot high chain-link fence around the vacant homes and the canal, built a drainage containment system twelve to twenty feet below the surface, and completed the permanent Love Canal Leachate Treatment Facility. During the ensuing cleanup activity, three hundred families living with a 10-block neighborhood were temporarily relocated as a result of health risks caused by chemical exposures. And in 1979, the U. S. Department of Justice filed a lawsuit against Hooker Chemical for the cost of the cleanup as well as punitive damages for harming the environment. The government's claims (which were joined by personal injury and property damage claims by area residents, by insurance company claims, and by the state of New York's demand for cleanup cost reimbursement) totaled a staggering $865 million dollars.

By the time 1980 rolled around, the U. S. Congress had passed the $1.6 billion "Superfund Act" which provided money to clean up chemical spills and toxic waste dumps all over the country. The Environmental Protection Agency had also conducted a study to determine the extent of contamination of air, water, and soil at the Love Canal site—as well as impacts on local residents. Blood tests eventually revealed that many residents had experienced chromosome damage that placed them at increased risks for cancer and reproductive problems.

During the decade of the 1980s, the following activity occurred: 789 homes were abandoned after being sold to the government; the 99th Street Elementary School was demolished; on-site water, gas, storm, and sanitary sewer lines were plugged with concrete; thousands of trees, shrubs, and topsoil were removed; a thick, high-density polyethylene liner was placed over 40 acres of the Love Canal site and compacted with eighteen inches of compacted soil fill—which was then seeded to provide a healthy vegetative cover; and finally, approximately 100 wells were drilled around the Love Canal site to provide a system of long-term monitoring.

In 1994, a federal judge ruled that Occidental Chemical Corporation was not liable for punitive damages in the Love Canal case. A year later, the U. S. Justice Department announced a final settlement wherein Occidental would pay $129 million in cleanup costs.

The Disaster Site Today

After studying the history of the Love Canal in great detail, I flew to Niagara Falls to see the site for myself. I rented a car and drove straight to a retirement community located immediately northwest of the canal. It had been there during the controversy, was still operational, and I figured I might be fortunate enough to meet some residents who had lived in the area since World War II. When I walked into the game room, people welcomed me cordially and offered to help in any way they could. Then one voice from the other side of the room raised above all the others.

"You want to know about the Love Canal?" he said. "I'm a former police officer and I've lived here my whole life. I'll tell you about the Love Canal."

This gentleman was an answer to my dreams. He and I jumped into his van and he informed me that he would take me on a driving tour of the entire site and, all along the way, he would be a walking encyclopedia of knowledge.

"The Love Canal is oriented in a north-south direction," he began. "I'll drive you around the entire thing. It'll take the rest of the day. You stop me if you have questions. We'll start by heading down the west side."

The only real residential development that had existed west of the Love Canal was a large low income neighborhood called the LaSalle public housing project. The entire thing had been bulldozed and demolished. Nothing was left but the concrete foundations of the projects and associated stores and

The Love Canal area today.

gas stations. My guide informed me that this development was one of the first places to be removed because the residents were more easily relocated.

The southern portion of the Love Canal is bordered by Lake Erie and there are only a couple hundred yards of land occupied, in part, by an east-west-running highway. As we drove along that road, I was struck by the closeness of the lake to the canal and equally amazed that there had never been any reported contamination to this huge body of water.

As we headed up the east side of the canal, we saw additional concrete slabs where drug stores, groceries, and businesses had once operated. Occasionally, the old store buildings were still standing but obviously long since abandoned. Then we drove into the old single family neighborhoods—all of which were still standing intact. The government had offered to purchase these homes and nearly everyone took advantage of the deal. So we were driving along rows and rows of deserted houses where no living thing was in sight. It was eerie—just like an old west ghost town.

Foundations of the prior developments to the west of the Love Canal containment area. The actual canal can be seen in the background.

Photo by Randall Bell

Then, suddenly, we came upon a house where there were cars in the driveway—and an American flag was flying in a well-manicured and landscaped yard.

"What's this?" I asked.

"This is the house of one of the seven homeowners who refused to accept the government's offer," replied my guide. "They never left."

"Holy mackerel," I remarked. "Where are the other six?"

"All scattered around. None of them are even close to each other."

We next headed into the neighborhoods on the north side of the Love Canal. These single-family homes were also bought out. However, subsequent environmental testing revealed that this area never really had a contamination problem. So, only a few years before, the government had actually fixed up the homes and started selling them back to the public. We stopped the van along one of the occupied streets and I shot

Photo by Randall Bell

Some of the hundreds of boarded up homes that line the streets to the east of the Love Canal containment area.

some videotape of children playing in their back yards. In the background is the old toxic dumpsite.

Today, that area is called the Love Canal Containment Area.

Nothing rests on the original sixteen-acre Love Canal which is a big grass-green berm enclosed by an eight-foot chain-link fence. Surrounding the canal is an additional sixty-acre buffer of open green space that includes sports fields. The 93rd Street Elementary School has long since been torn down and the only structure within the containment area is a small pumping station that basically removes any contamination that leaches out to the perimeter.

Authorities never tried to remove all the toxic chemicals. The whole idea was to keep them contained and implement an extensive ongoing program to monitor the groundwater table and assure the integrity of the containment area. In this way, the Love Canal is expected to remain in perpetuity forever.

Impact and Insight

The residential subdivision to the north of the Love Canal is called Black Creek Village and, as I mentioned, was renovated and sold back to the public house by house. In order to move the properties, the government initially offered 20 percent discounts. Over the years, the discount was dropped to 15 percent, then to 10 and 5 percent. By the year 2000, people were paying full market value for the homes. Today, Black Creek Village is a very nice bread and butter neighborhood.

On both the west and east sides of the canal, the city of Niagara Falls and the Town of Wheatfield have joined together and are planning to develop a commercial and light industrial park complex. In general, all the area the Environmental Protection Agency studied and found to be hazardous to human health will not be allowed to develop in a residential manner. Abandoned homes on the east side will be torn down and the seven occupied residential houses will be offered buyouts. Because industrial parks have building footprints with concrete foundations, asphalt parking, and green areas that are not occupied—any possible contamination is capped over. In the long run, the development of the industrial complex along the sides of the Love Canal will become a very lucrative endeavor. Essentially, the property will sell for full value.

So the longest-running case study in environmental pollution demonstrates that even large-scale contamination sites don't create areas of indefinite blight. Basically, usage may change from residential to industrial. People adjust and life moves on.

Lessons Learned

1. Listen to the Experts and Be Teachable

The Love Canal disaster was caused by an ignorant and "unteachable" board of education. The board disregarded expert advice, built an elementary school on the filled-in portion of the canal, and actively encouraged residential development in close proximity to the site. It was an incredibly stupid decision.

The lesson to be learned here is straightforward. It does not matter how many Ph.D.s you possess, or what kind of education you have. If you believe you're above seeking and taking the advice of experts, then you are going to make uninformed and unwise decisions.

People with expertise in a given field need to be consulted and heard, and their advice should be followed—especially in professions where human health and welfare are concerned. Ironically, Hooker Chemical Company (Occidental) was sued but the board of education was not. It should have been the other way around.

2.   When Motivated by Money and Emotion, Step Back and Count to 100

The board of education was motivated by self-interest. They saw an opportunity to acquire a lot of land for a very cheap price. They put their self-interest above reason, in part, because they let their emotions carry them away.

The Love Canal had been sitting there for decades. There was no excuse for rushing into a potentially dangerous situation. The board had plenty of time to consider all the facts and potential consequences. Everybody involved needed to step back and take time to think about what they were considering.

3

Bombing of the Murrah Federal Building
Oklahoma City, Oklahoma
April 19, 1995

The Disaster

It occurred in the middle of the week, a Wednesday morning, the beginning of a new day. Five hundred people routinely filed into the Alfred P. Murrah Federal Building at the corner of 5th Street and Harvey Avenue on the edge of downtown Oklahoma City. They worked for federal government agencies such as the Bureau of Alcohol, Tobacco and Firearms, the Drug Enforcement Administration, the Secret Service, Housing and Urban Development, Social Security, Veterans Affairs, a federal credit union, and several military recruiting offices. Many parents dropped off their preschool-age children at America's Kids, a daycare center located on the northwest side of the second floor. And nearly everybody was at their desk when the day officially started at 9:00 AM.

Right about then, a terrorist parked a rental truck in front of the main entrance on the north side of the building. The cargo portion of the truck was packed with twelve hundred pounds of ammonium nitrate (a common farm fertilizer) mixed with fuel oil. That combination is known to produce an incredibly powerful explosion when detonated.

The terrorist walked a couple of blocks away and ducked behind a building. At 9:03 AM, he ignited the bomb. A reddish-orange fireball blasted skyward and dark black cloud of debris filled the air. The blast left a crater twenty feet wide and eight feet deep where the rental truck was parked. One of the wheel axles was later found two blocks away. Windows were blown out in buildings within a five-mile radius. Automobiles parked on the streets nearby burst into flames. The shock wave from the explosion was felt more than thirty miles away.

When the smoke cleared, the north half of the nine-story Murrah building was gone—it had been blown away. As the front support columns were destroyed, floors collapsed upon each other. Cables and air ducts dangled from the wreckage. Splintered furniture and shattered bricks flew in all directions. People who survived the blast ran for their lives. When rescuers arrived on the scene, they found mass confusion and what looked like a war zone. They saw the mangled bodies of the adult employees who worked in the building and of the children who had been playing at the daycare center. Survivors staggered around bloodied and battered. Countless other people were trapped under the masses of concrete and steel. By the end of the day, sixty trapped people had been rescued from the rubble, nineteen adults and twelve

The Alfred P. Murrah Federal Building shortly after the explosion.

White House photo by Paul Morse

children were confirmed dead, and three hundred people were unaccounted for.

The governor of Oklahoma declared a state of emergency and the National Guard was sent in. News media from all over the world descended on Oklahoma City. Reporters, camera people, news vans, and satellite dishes cluttered the streets for two city blocks around the disaster site. Over the next two weeks, bodies of men, women, and children continued to be pulled from the rubble. The final count determined that 168 people had lost their lives and hundreds more had been seriously injured.

Timothy McVeigh, arrested and convicted for bombing the Murrah Federal Building.

The Oklahoma Highway Patrol immediately issued an all-points bulletin for suspects. Ninety minutes after the explosion, the terrorist, driving north to Kansas at 90 miles per hour, was pulled over by an officer for speeding and driving without a license plate. He was an American associated with a group that had antigovernment sentiments. Tried and convicted, he was later executed for the crime.

The Disaster Site Today

Every disaster has two elements: the emotional side and the practical real estate side. When I visited Oklahoma City a few months after the tragedy, I was overwhelmed emotionally. The balance of the federal building had already been demolished. The area was fenced in, the grounds bulldozed, and a grass lawn had been planted. When I turned the corner on 5th Street and viewed the site for the first time, it hit me like a ton of bricks. On the chain-link fence surrounding the site were thousands of photos, letters, flowers, Teddy Bears, dolls, and other items that had belonged to the victims.

I'm not a particularly emotional person, but every person present (and there were lots of people there) was in tears. It was an unbelievably sad and tragic feeling. As a matter of fact, I was not able to concentrate on doing my job until the next day.

It was news to me, until I got there, that the damage from the bomb was very widespread and not limited to the Murrah Building. Many other structures in the area had sustained major structural damage. Buildings to the north, east, and west, including the YMCA, the Regency Towers Apartments, several churches, and a U.S. post office—all within a block of the disaster site—were damaged to the point that they were later torn down, repaired, or reconstructed.

On the other hand, areas to the south of the explosion remained relatively unscathed. The three-story parking facility (which was attached to the Murrah Building) still stands today and is used in conjunction with the federal courthouse, which also suffered only minor damage. The rooftop terraces on top

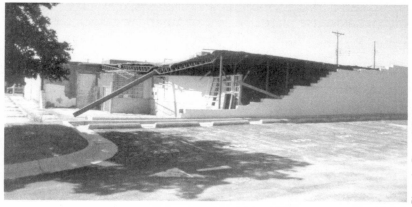

Photo by Randall Bell

Bomb damage located blocks away from the Alfred P. Murrah Federal Building.

of the parking structure (which includes plants, trees, park benches, and picnic tables that were used by the Murrah federal employees) are also still there.

Traffic on 5th Street has been permanently closed and a memorial has been built. Today, the disaster site is a national memorial that honors victims, survivors, and rescuers of the tragedy. The three-acre setting includes a reflecting pool, a children's area, an orchard, a "Survivor Tree," a memorial fence, and 168 "floating" chairs in memory of the victims.

Impact and Insight

Ironically, a lot of disasters do not necessarily spell out financial disaster for everyone. Many times, real estate is destroyed and, on the emotional side, there's nothing good to say about it. On the practical real estate side, however, often what has been destroyed is rebuilt with insurance dollars and ends up much better than it was in the first place. I call this "The Santa Claus Factor." And part of what happened in the aftermath of the Oklahoma City bombing is a good example of it.

Photo by Randall Bell

A damaged church located directly across the street from the Alfred P. Murrah Federal Building.

Northwest 5th Street, where the Murrah Federal Building was situated, turned out to be kind of a dividing line. The bomb exploded on the north side, which is where the blown-out shell of the building was. Most of the damage to surrounding property occurred north of that line. Many of the structures were rebuilt. As a matter of fact, the federal government purchased numerous destroyed properties and put forth plans to construct a low-rise building "campus" complex that will be a model for future government complexes which, of course, will provide a deterrent to devastating attacks in the future. In the end, these property values went up considerably.

South of the site is a nice, high-end business district with lots of office buildings and restaurants. For the most part, it was relatively unharmed and has maintained its real estate value. In the long run, it will most likely rise due to the national memorial nearby. The site now draws tourists—pilgrims, if you will. When tourists visit Oklahoma City, one of the things they do is go to

Photo by Randall Bell

A chain-link fence, which served as a temporary memorial, surrounded the Alfred P. Murrah Federal Building site prior to the eventual construction of a formal memorial.

the memorial. And we all know that tourist attractions posi- tively influence the overall economy. And that, of course, leads to higher real estate values.

As far as the three acres of the disaster site, the real estate value is both valueless and priceless. Technically, the value of the land goes to zero because it will never again be developed for commercial, residential, or private. The museum charges admission, which creates value. But a price cannot be put on the national memorial. It is, and always will be, hallowed ground—with a special place in American history and in the hearts of Americans everywhere.

Lessons Learned
1.   Federal Government Facilities Should Be Low Rise and Campuslike
When the Alfred P. Murrah Federal Building was constructed, national terrorism was not in the forefront of concern. As a result of the disaster, there was a fundamental alteration of future building plans from the federal government.

Policy makers realized that government facilities would be targets for future terrorist attacks. So they put in place plans to avoid the high-rise, singular building architectural concept and replaced it with multiple, low-rise, cluster-type campuses.

2.   The Reality Is That Some Man-Made Disasters Can- not Be Prevented
Some disasters are going to hit us and we really don't know what could have been done to prevent them. There are groups of people who have tremendous resentment against our nation. Some terrorist acts are going to happen because of evil minds. We cannot always foretell these kinds of disasters. So we should avoid our natural tendency to pin blame on people or agencies that are, in fact, victims.

4

Nuclear Weapons Testing on Bikini and Enewetak Atolls

The Marshall Islands; Pacific Ocean
June 1946–March 1958

The Disaster

Shortly after World War II, the United States began what was to become the most extensive program of nuclear weapons testing in recorded history. For both security and safety reasons, two remote locations in the Marshall Islands were selected for the experiments—the first of which was dubbed "Operation Crossroads." The Marshall Islands, located in the Pacific Ocean along the equator, is a small nation comprised of twenty-nine atolls scattered over approximately 375,000 square miles. The two areas selected were the Bikini and Enewetak atolls.

Local residents were informed by representatives of the U.S. government that they would be helping mankind by vacating their islands for a few months while the bombs were being detonated. With no resources or detailed knowledge of what this all meant, the local islanders accepted everything that was said to them at face value. So, in March 1946, 167 islanders on Bikini (and, later, a similar number on Enewetak) were relocated 125 miles east to other atolls. Four months later, the nuclear weapons testing began.

The first two devices detonated were similar in size to those dropped on Hiroshima and Nagasaki, Japan at the end of World War II. The explosions were so powerful and illuminated the sky to such an extent that French clothing designers later named their scant new swimsuits "bikinis" after the "sensational bombshells" at the Bikini Atoll.

Over the next eight years, eleven similar nuclear weapons were detonated on the Bikini and Enewetak atolls. Then, in 1954, preparations began for the testing of a series of megaton-range bombs, including America's first deliverable hydrogen bomb—which was expected to cause much greater destruction. Just how much larger, however, was unknown at the time. For a variety of reasons, the first such test, named "Bravo," turned out to be a singular event that created terrible, long-lasting problems.

Normally, prevailing winds in the Marshall Islands blow westward out to the open sea. But on February 28, the eve of the Bravo test, weather reports indicated that atmospheric conditions were "less than favorable" because the winds had shifted eastward. This meant that the nuclear fallout would go directly over inhabited islands.

At midnight, just seven hours prior to the scheduled detonation, official weather reports related that there were "less than favorable winds at 10,000- to 25,000-foot levels" and they "were headed for Rongelap [Atoll] to the east." For reasons that no one has ever adequately explained, the test was not canceled—and several Navy vessels were quickly ordered out of the expected fallout zone.

At 7:00 o'clock on the morning of March 1, 1954, the hydrogen bomb, "Bravo," was detonated on the surface of the reef in the northwestern corner of Bikini Atoll. This explosion turned out to be the single largest nuclear blast ever detonated on the surface of the earth. A huge flash of blinding light and a raging fireball of heat that measured into the millions of degrees shot skyward at a rate of three hundred miles per hour. Millions of tons of sand, coral, plants, and sea life from Bikini's reef, and from three islands and the surrounding lagoon waters, were instantly vaporized. Left behind was a crater more than one mile wide and 400 feet deep. The blast was three times larger than expected and scientists were simply stunned when they realized that Bravo turned out to be a thousand times more powerful than the bombs dropped on Hiroshima and Nagasaki. The resulting radioactive fallout was equally more extensive. Radioactive monitors on board Navy ships located to the south of Bikini became so high that all sailors were ordered below decks and all hatches and watertight doors were closed.

Meanwhile, 125 miles east on Rongelap Atoll, an islander named Nelson had just gotten up and was making a pot of coffee when he saw the fireball from the blast on the horizon. Shortly thereafter, he felt the shock wave on his face and noticed six-foot waves rolling into the lagoon. Three to four hours later, a gritty white, snowlike ash began to fall from the sky. The radioactive dust formed a brackish-yellow layer on the freshwater ponds used for drinking water. And Nelson's daughter, along with a couple of dozen children, played and danced in the fallout.

That night many of those children and other residents of Rongelap became nauseous and started vomiting. They developed skin burns and their hair fell out. Within seventy-two hours, the islanders were evacuated to safety and placed under medical care. At the same time, the Atomic Energy Commission issued a public statement calling the Bravo test a "routine atomic test," and stated that some of the Marshallese people were "unexpectedly exposed to some radioactivity," that there "were no burns," and that "all [the people] were reported well."

Above and on facing page is a series of photographs of an underwater explosion of a 21 kiloton atomic bomb during Operation Crossroads (Event Baker), conducted at Bikini Atoll on June 30, 1946.

Meanwhile, many of the project scientists expressed excitement by the fact that the islanders were exposed to the nuclear fallout. Now they would be able to study the long-term effects of radioactivity on humans. The islanders were then resettled on contaminated islands so they could be evaluated for their reactions to the radiation.

Over the next several decades, Marshallese people were moved back and forth among the exposed atolls. But, in 1978, when an Interior Department study found that there was a 75 percent increase in radioactive cesium in the bodies of Bikini islanders, the government moved everybody off the atoll immediately and, this time, kept them off. About that same time, more than 700 military personnel participated in a nuclear "cleanup" of Enewetak Atoll where more than 250,000 cubic yards of soil and debris were dumped into a bomb crater and sealed with a cap of cement.

Nuclear weapons testing in the Marshall Islands ended on August 18, 1958 after a total of sixty-six bombs had been detonated. A five-year study of 432 islands in the Marshall Islands revealed that almost half of this small nation was dusted by radioactive fallout. Forced to acknowledge the impact, the U.S. government paid, via trust funds, several hundred million dollars in reparations to the impacted islanders.

The Disaster Site Today

I first visited the disaster site as a consultant to the Nuclear Claims Tribunal and the people of Rongelap Atoll. When I arrived at the capital city of Majaro, I was picked up at the airport and given a quick tour of the local atoll.

The first observation I made was that the Marshall Islands are a fragile place. There is nearly no distinction between land and sea. The average elevation is a mere seven feet above sea level, so there are no hills, mountains, or valleys. As a matter of fact, when we crossed a small, elevated bridge, I was informed by my guide that we were now at the highest point in the entire nation.

Land is also scarce there. The atolls consist of a series of long islands and reefs that surround a lagoon. In many areas, there is a small two-lane road with houses on either side and the houses themselves front either the lagoon or the ocean. Indeed, in many areas, the island was so narrow that I was able to throw a rock from the ocean to the lagoon.

Photo by Randall Bell

The "Bravo Crater" was created when the infamous Bravo Test was conducted. The nuclear explosion vaporized two and one-half islands and left a crater one mile wide and 400 feet deep.

The second day on location, I took an airplane tour over the Bikini and Enewetak atolls. From the air, Bikini looks like a tropical moon—round craters all over the place filled with lush green vegetation and, every now and then, a concrete bunker that once housed testing equipment. The crater made from the Bravo Test is enormous—about a mile in diameter and nearly a perfect circle filled with deep blue tropical waters.

From the air, another most unusual phenomenon is also visible. All of the palm trees line up in straight rows like Kansas wheat field. There were so many bombs dropped on Bikini and Enewetak that virtually every piece of vegetation was obliterated. Before nuclear testing, the coconut was not only a food staple, it provided a natural industry to the Marshall Islands. Most notably, the dried meat of the mature coconut was grown commercially for its oils and was also used to create various natural soaps. In an effort to make up for the loss, the United States government planted rows and rows of new coconut trees in precise military-type straight lines all over the islands.

Seeing those trees planted in precisely straight lines is a somewhat paradoxical sight—especially when you take into account

The concrete cap built over the dump site on Enewetak to contain radioactive waste.

that, from the ground, the Enewetak Atoll, along with the Bikini Atoll, is an incredibly beautiful place. They are lush, tropical, island paradises replete with untouched sand beaches, exotic tropical fish, large sea turtles, coconut crabs, and palm trees.

Equally beautiful are the atolls that were not bombed, but experienced only radioactive fallout. And yet, there also, the paradox exists with remnants of abandoned buildings that indicate a once happy lifestyle. On Rongelap, we needed machetes to cut our way through dense jungle in order to reach several old houses and churches. I went into one little chapel where psalm books and Bibles were lying open on the pews. It was apparent that people got the order to evacuate and just got up and walked out.

Sadly, people were not allowed to return to Bikini and Enewetak until the year 2000—and, even then, only in certain places. So, in reality, those few months they were asked to evacuate their homes back in 1946 turned into fifty-four years—more than half a century.

Today, the people residing on all these exposed islands live a different lifestyle. They cannot live off the land, so canned food goods are flown in by the U.S. government on a regular basis. Many people now live in a perpetual welfare state where alcoholism, teen-age pregnancy, and other social problems are commonplace. Others, however, continue to be productive by turning out handmade crafts (such as baskets and artwork) and selling them to tourists.

Everywhere you walk on the impacted islands, you are reminded of the radioactivity of the place. You see adults with "nuclear necklaces" who, when they were kids had their thyroids taken out because the nuclear fallout caused them to get cancer. You see trees marked with DOE (Department of Energy) tags that regularly measure their radioactivity. On Bikini and Rongelap, you run across small buildings where islanders go for regular body scans that measure their exposure to radiation. And on Enewetak, there is a huge mound called "The Dome." Those 250,000 yards of soil and debris that were scraped together came from four inches of soil off the top of the entire atoll. While initially dumped into one of the bomb craters, there was so much radioactive material that it built up into a ten-foot "dome" that was capped in concrete.

Children are more vulnerable to radiation exposure because their central nervous system is not fully developed. With adults, however, it takes about thirty years for exposure to radiation to develop into full-blown cancer. Nearly 70 percent of the Rongelap children under ten years old who were exposed to radiation from the Bravo test developed thyroid cancer. Many later died, including Nelson's daughter. At the turn of the twenty-first century, the incidence of thyroid cancer in the Marshall Islands was reported to be 100 times higher than anywhere else in the world.

On Bikini, Enewetak, Rongelap, and the other impacted atolls, annual exposure to a person who lives there year around exceeds 1,700 millirems of radiation—more than a hundred times the maximum safe level. In order to counter the impact, the top twelve inches of soil (where most of the radioactive nuclides are concentrated) is treated with a potassium fertilizer that reduces the radioactive food chain dose by 90 percent over five years. One also can observe large open areas filled with gravel, which acts as a buffer between the people and radioactive soil. Also, because natural groundwater is too contaminated to drink, large water containment cisterns are scattered throughout the atolls. And people are told that nobody is to eat off the land because anything like coconuts, pandanus, and breadfruit are too contaminated for safe consumption.

Interestingly enough, though, because the lagoons are purged by the oceans two to three times each year, fish can be safely consumed. As a result, sport fishing—swordfish, marlin, deep-sea fishing—is very popular in the Marshall Islands, especially off the Bikini Atoll. As a matter of fact, it is considered by many as the number one scuba diving sight in the world. Not only are there tons of sea life, but there are dozens of shipwrecks all around the area—which adds to a world-class diving experience. These shipwrecks, however, are not ancient. They are dozens of U.S. Navy vessels that were sunk during the nuclear testing. The USS Saratoga, for instance, is one of many vessels resting at 150-foot depths off the Bikini Atoll.

Impact and Insight

As anyone might imagine, the impact of having more than five dozen nuclear bombs detonated in your backyard is devastating. First of all, land was not only vaporized, it was contaminated by radioactive fallout to the point that, in some places, it cannot be used for anything at all. Second, the nation's natural coconut industry was virtually obliterated because no other country in the world will accept exported coconuts from the Marshall Islands—not even from the hundreds of islands that are not affected by radiation. But measuring that impact on real estate, in a hard-number, quantifiable way, was extraordinarily difficult. It was, by far, the most complex evaluation challenge I have ever experienced.

The people of the Marshall Islands have a sacred respect for their land. They believe it to have been inhabited by their ancestors since time began. Their social status is tied directly to their land rights—as is their capacity to earn income through the sale of related coconut products, etc. Moreover, tradition dictates that property be handed down from generation to generation through the maternal bloodline. So land is owned by a single family that goes back no less than a couple of centuries—long before any written records were kept. But even if sufficient records did exist, they would have been virtually useless in the cases of Bikini and Enewetak because land was completely obliterated or the topography had changed so that boundaries could not be measured accurately.

In determining monetary damages for our clients, we benchmarked all our calculations on two things. First was on the rule of thumb that, in terms of finance, a property owned for a period of thirty years (given the time value of money) is equivalent to the full value of the real estate. Second, on several contracts with the United States government in which the Marshall Islands leased a significant amount of property for use as a strategic military outpost in the Pacific Ocean. The lease provide us with a financial foundation from which to work and our interpolations and allowed us to come up with a justifiable figure.

In the end, we concluded that land (in terms of square mileage) on the Bikini Atoll was rendered nonuseable for real estate purposes for a minimum period of forty years. Over that timeframe, the impact on real estate (accumulated plus interest) amounted to more than one billion dollars.

Lessons Learned

1. Always Be Prepared to Stop the Train

The worst part of the entire disaster related to nuclear weapons testing on the Bikini and Enewetak atolls occurred during the events leading up to the Bravo Test. When the prevailing winds changed toward the inhabited islands, it shouldn't have taken a genius to realize that an atomic bomb should not have been detonated that day. But the train was headed down the tracks at full speed and nobody wanted to stop it.

Government officials during this historical event had tremendous authority, but they were not above the very human tendency to duck, run, hide, and deny. Had they not detonated the bomb that day, authorities would not have been put in a position where they had to protect their own self interests.

There's no group of people, no matter how high on the totem pole, who should not be prepared to stop a major event should conditions change and cause danger to other human beings. That kind of abhorrent behavior will eventually come back to bite you. And the American government found that out when it had to spend billions of dollars in repairs, reparations, and punitive damages.

1. To Err Is Human, to Forgive Divine

With the exception of the Bravo test, most officials in charge of the experiments were unaware of the terrible consequences that would result from nuclear testing in the Marshall Islands. And even in the Bravo case, the long-term effects of radiation exposure were not known.

To tell you the truth, I was a little concerned about going on location because I'm an American and I thought the people would be angry with me. But the Marshallese are not an angry people. On the contrary, they are kind, courteous, pleasant, and openly forgiving.

It is that sense of forgiveness, I believe, that helps them move on with life. And it was that sense of forgiveness that put me at ease and made me feel comfortable among people I had never met.

After all they had been through, the people of the Marshall Islands were at peace with both themselves and the world the world around them. I felt good when I was among them. I felt blessed. And for the first time, I believed that, as Alexander Pope said, forgiveness really is divine.

5

Murders of Nicole Brown Simpson and Ron Goldman

875 South Bundy Drive, West Los Angeles, California
June 12, 1994

The Disaster

The brutal crime that led to what has been dubbed the "Trial of the Century" took place just inside the front gate of a four-bedroom condominium in the quiet and prestigious community of West Los Angeles, California. The victims were Nicole Brown Simpson and her friend, Ron Goldman. The accused was famed football player, actor, and celebrity, O. J. Simpson.

Considered one of the greatest running backs in football history, Simpson had won the prestigious Heisman Trophy as the best player in college football and then went on to a hall-of-fame career in the National Football League. Since 1979, he had been a successful sports commentator and actor.

After a turbulent twelve-year marriage, Simpson and Nicole were divorced less than two years prior to the murders. He lived in a house on Rockingham Drive just a few miles from 875 South Bundy Drive where

Nicole Brown Simpson

she and their two children resided. At the time of the crime, Nicole's condominium was for sale because she wanted to move farther away from Simpson. According to her parents and sisters, Nicole was afraid for her life.

At 6:30 PM on the evening of June 12, 1994, Nicole and her family dined together at the Mezzaluna Restaurant—a few blocks away from her condo. Upon returning home, Nicole's mother, Juditha, realized she had accidentally left her prescription eyeglasses at the restaurant. The glasses were soon located and Ron Goldman, a waiter at Mezzaluna and friend of Nicole, offered to walk them over to her place as soon as his shift was over.

After dinner, Nicole and her two children, Sydney and Justin, stopped off at Ben & Jerry's for some take-out ice cream and then headed home. The children soon finished off their desserts and got ready for bed. Nicole drew a hot bath and, as was her habit, lit candles around the tub. Meanwhile, twenty-three-year-old Ron Goldman, clocked out of Mezzaluna at 9:45

The site of the murders on Bundy Street.

Photo by Randall Bell

and, carrying an envelope containing Mrs. Brown's eyeglasses, started his walk toward Bundy Drive.

Nicole was sitting out near the garage finishing up her ice cream when the buzzer on the intercom went off. Realizing it was Ron, Nicole set her ice cream down and walked through the house toward the front gate to let him in.

According to police files and court records, the police believe O. J. Simpson was hiding out on the front patio. Carrying a knife and wearing a wool hat and gloves, Simpson, police speculate, was peering through the window and over an inside credenza, when Nicole walked out. They believe that when he saw his ex-wife come outside and start down the dimly lit, Spanish tile walkway to let in a handsome young man, he became enraged and all hell broke loose.

The following scenario was put forth by the prosecution during the trial: Simpson attacked Nicole and stabbed her four times in the left side of her neck and three times in the back of her head. In the process, her black cocktail dress was ripped and she placed her hands in a defensive position to try and ward off the attack. Incapacitated, Nicole slumped to the ground.

Standing at the gate, Ron Goldman yelled, "Hey! Hey! Hey!" and rushed to Nicole's rescue. Ron then got into a life or death fight with Simpson while Nicole's dog, Kato, barked wildly. Overpowered by the larger and stronger athlete, Ron's neck was slashed several times on both sides, and he was stabbed three times in the chest, once in the abdomen, and once in the thigh. His hands also suffered numerous cuts. During this struggle, O. J. Simpson's wool hat and left-hand glove came off and fell to the ground. Simpson suffered only a small wound on his left middle index finger. But Ron Goldman was killed—and he slumped to the ground, his back against a tree stump, with the envelope containing Juditha Brown's glasses lying near his knees.

Simpson, in a blind rage, then went back and finished off Nicole. He slit her throat from the left side of her neck to her right ear two and one half inches deep—all the way through her spinal column—and left her lying on the walkway in a pool of blood. Simpson next made a beeline for his home on Rockingham Drive in Brentwood. He parked his white Bronco askew to the curb at a side entrance and slipped into the compound. At the front driveway gate, a limousine driver had been waiting to pick up Simpson and drive him to the airport to catch a plane for a planned trip to Chicago. The driver had shown up twenty minutes early and had repeatedly rung the buzzer—but no one had answered. In order not to be seen by the limo driver, Simpson ran along the outer back wall of his guesthouse. Because it was late at night and dark, he accidentally crashed into the air conditioning unit and fell to the ground. In that fall, Simpson dropped his right-hand glove. Inside the guesthouse, house guest Kato Kaelin heard the noise and went outside to investigate. Kaelin, himself, did not see Simpson but, from the front gate, the limo driver saw Kaelin with a flashlight. Moments later, he spotted what he later described as a six-foot-tall black person wearing dark clothes enter the house through the front door. Lights then went on in the foyer and the rest of the house. The next time the driver rang the buzzer, Simpson answered and said that he had fallen asleep but would be out in a few minutes to go to the airport.

Shortly after Simpson's plane took off for Chicago at 11:45 PM, Nicole's dog led some neighbors to the murder scene on Bundy Drive. Police were then called in to

The entire nation watched the slow speed Bronco "chase" on national television.

investigate one of the most gruesome killings in Los Angeles history. That investigation, in turn, led to the murder trial of O. J. Simpson—a national drama that lasted more than a year, from July 1994 to September 1995.

The Los Angeles district attorney's office presented what it termed, "a mountain of evidence" to prove its two-count murder one indictments. Among the most compelling evidence were the DNA blood matches that linked Simpson to the crimes. They found Nicole's blood on both of Simpson's socks, Ron Goldman's blood inside the glove found at Simpson's home, and Simpson's blood at both the crime scene and his Rockingham estate. Simpson's defense team of high-profile attorneys and experts was quickly dubbed "The Dream Team." They strung out the trial, challenged police investigative techniques, discredited one police detective on racial bias, and cast doubt on both physical and eyewitness evidence. In the end, O. J. Simpson was found not guilty on both counts.

Simpson and attorney Shapiro

The Disaster Site Today

During the trial, I was asked by Nicole's father, Lou Brown, to measure the economic impact that the crime scene stigma had on the Bundy property. I met and interacted with Mr. Brown, his immediate family, the listing real estate agent, and the individual who eventually purchased the property.

I personally walked the crime scene many times and saw all the things I had heard about in the news. I saw the ring left by Nicole's ice cream cup on the ledge by the garage. I stood on the front patio where police believe that Simpson hid and spied through the window. I strolled the walkway where the murders occurred. I stood by the tree where Ron Goldman's body was found. And I saw the candles still in the exact places by Nicole's bathtub. It was a very moving, emotional experience for me.

Bundy Drive in West Los Angeles, being a major off-ramp from I-10, is an extremely busy street. Right after the murders, thousands of people showed up and just stood around staring at the crime scene—and it is still a place that tourists visit on a regular basis. The residence, itself, is legally a condo, but it's really more of a duplex—having a common wall with another home. It was inherently designed to buffer against any kind of street noise and is well insulated from the outside world. From the Bundy Drive side, there is a long walkway, bounded by thick vegetation on both sides, leading up to a steel fence and gate that blocks any entry from the general public. Beyond the gate, the walkway continues until it reaches the residence. Then there are steps up to the little patio where police say Simpson was hiding.

Two and one-half years after the murders (more than a year and a half after the trial ended), the property was purchased by a very nice professional couple. They asked my advice and I suggested they change both the address and the facade on Bundy Drive which, I believed, would keep the gawking down. Some months later, I was working on an environmental case at the corner of Wilshire Boulevard and Bundy Drive and became curious to see if my advice had been followed.

So I drove up the street, and although I had been to the condo many times, I drove right past it because it was no longer recognizable to me. I parked my car and then walked along the sidewalk until I found the entrance. The address had, indeed, been changed—and the facade had been very tastefully redone. The steel gate had also been replaced with a seven-foot-high, wood, stockade-type fence—and now no one could even see the condo. While I was standing on the sidewalk contemplating all of the changes, a bus full of tourists from Florida pulled up, unloaded, and people started snapping pictures of the condo next door. I chuckled to myself and then got back in my car and drove off.

Today, tour groups still stop by and snap pictures of the wrong condo. Other than that, Bundy Drive is just another bustling artery off I-10. For the most part, the gawking has cooled off.

Impact and Insight

Every disaster has both a practical side and a tragic side. In this case, I've already spelled out the tragic side. On the practical side, the Brown family needed to sell Nicole's condo—so that's what I focused on. At the time of the murders, the property was listed for a selling price of approximately $650,000. According to Lou Brown, Nicole was afraid for her safety and felt she had to move farther away from her ex-husband. Now, he wanted to know if the property was worth more or less than the price for which Nicole had it listed.

In determining a new estimated value for the property, I studied other famous crime scenes all across the country. Among the most interesting was the nearby property in Benedict Canyon where Sharon Tate and her friends were murdered by followers of Charles Manson. The crime had occurred on August 9, 1969 and, interestingly enough, Sharon Tate and her husband, Roman Polansky, did not own the home. They were renters. After the killings, the owner moved back into the house and made no attempt to sell it. Twenty-two years later, in 1991, the property sold at full market value. Although nobody had forgotten about Charles Manson, enough time had passed so that the stigma of the crime (in terms of its impact on real estate) had gone away entirely.

I determined that this would also be the case for the crime scene on Bundy Drive. I advised Mr. Brown that, in the immediate aftermath of the tragedy (one to two years), the property would most likely see a 10 to 25 percent decrease in value. With time, though, that diminution would gradually decrease and the market value would go back up.

Mr. Brown did sell the condo at 875 South Bundy Drive. With time, the property got right back into the flow of the regular market.

Lessons Learned

1. Take Preventative Action When There Are Early Warning Signals

As hard as this is to say, there were numerous warning signals before this tragedy occurred. There was spousal abuse in the marriage, harassment after the divorce, a very disturbing 911 call for police help, and numerous incidents of Nicole's ex-husband stalking and spying on her.

The tragedy is amplified by the fact that Nicole, her friends, her family, and the police (although all were very concerned) did not do more to get her out of the situation in which she found herself—in terms of getting farther away and protecting her from her ex-husband. Had decisive and protective action been taken earlier, two very tragic murders may very well have been averted.

2.   A Terrible Tragedy May Be Turned Into Something Positive

One afternoon, while I was working with Lou Brown, I stopped by his office to drop off some material for him. Not intending to see him, I brought along my one-year-old daughter for the short ride. But Lou happened to be in the reception area when I passed through—and he came over to say hello. When he saw my daughter, a big smile came over his face and he picked her up and started to make her giggle. When I saw Lou holding my child, the entire tragedy came home to me in a very personal way. I could not imagine losing my daughter the way he had lost his. And for the first time, I think, I got a glimpse of the grief that he and his family had gone through.

Lou Brown and his family had suffered a triple tragedy. First, they had lost Nicole. Second, the man that a civil court had found responsible for the death of Nicole and Ron Goldman, had been freed after the criminal trial. And third, in a custody battle for Nicole's two children, the judge awarded the two children to O. J. Simpson rather than the Browns.

Many families would have been irreparably crushed by such a set of circumstances. But the Browns channeled all their grief into something really positive. They created the Nicole Brown Charitable Foundation—an organization that raises money for abused women. Most importantly, I believe, the Brown family raised public awareness of a very important social problem. They spoke publicly about what had happened to Nicole, about what the warning signs were, and about what actions should have been taken to prevent the ultimate tragedy. In doing so, the Browns helped countless women gain both the courage and the means to move away from an abusive husband. Previously, this was not a topic of discussion in the United States. Now it is openly talked about and widely recognized.

It takes incredible character to do what the Brown family did. By their example, they taught us all that, if we care and if we are strong, some of the best changes might result from some of the worst disasters.

6

Mount St. Helens Volcanic Eruption
Cascade Mountain Range, Washington
May 18, 1980

The Disaster

One of the most spectacular and destructive natural disasters in the history of the United States occurred on May 18, 1980 when the Mount St. Helens volcano erupted in southwestern Washington State. In a matter of minutes, it caused death, destruction, the loss of tens of thousands of fish and wildlife, and hundreds of miles of road and bridge infrastructure. It also resulted in, quite literally, the complete obliteration of hundreds of millions of dollars of real estate.

If anything can be said regarding good fortune in the face of such a disaster, it is that Mount St. Helens is situated in a relatively sparsely populated area of Washington. One hundred and twenty-five miles west of Yakima, and sixty miles north of Vancouver, there were really no towns or cities in the immediate vicinity. The developed area consisted mostly of mountain cabins and vacation retreats. The most significant of these areas was located ten miles north-northeast at Spirit Lake where a number of resorts and campgrounds ringed the shoreline.

Another point of good fortune was the fact that the smoldering volcano gave plenty of warning signals of the disaster that was about to take place. Dormant for more than a century, Mount St. Helens awoke on March 20, 1980 with a 4.2 magnitude earthquake. One week later, an explosion of steam blasted a 250-foot-wide crater through the snowcap. By early April, several dozen more explosions had expanded the crater to more than a thousand feet. Within three weeks, a mile and a half wide area, known as "The Bulge" had formed from the rise of ash and molten rock within the volcano's deep-seated vent. Scientists were certain that a huge eruption was about to take place. Accordingly, warnings were issued and everyone was advised to evacuate the area immediately. Most heeded the advice and got out. Some, however, absolutely refused to leave.

The scientists were correct in their predictions. At 8:32 AM on the morning of May 18, 1980, shortly after a 5.0 magnitude earthquake, Mount St. Helens erupted. The entire north side of the mountain blew off and volcanic ash towered sixteen miles high in the sky. The resulting explosion was equivalent to 27,000 atomic bombs. It was heard in Montana, Idaho, Northern California, British Columbia, and in small towns as far as seven hundred miles away.

Dept. of Natural Resources, State of Washington & NOAA

The Eruption of Mt. St. Helens on May 18, 1980 sent an eruptive cloud to an altitude of more than twelve miles in ten minutes. Ash particles from the cloud started forest fires.

Shortly after the vertical eruption began, a horizontal shock wave similar to that associated with a nuclear explosion rushed down the Toutle River Valley. At speeds as high as 670 miles per hour, hot gasses, searing volcanic ash, molten magma, and rocks were propelled northward wiping out virtually everything in the pathway. As this material progressed from the center of the eruption, it formed the largest recorded landslide in the history of the world—leaving a trail of debris eighteen miles long. It flattened forests—snapping off trees and scattering them like toothpicks. It "exploded" when it hit valleys in the topography and then "burst" as high as sixty feet into the air when it hit hills.

At Spirit Lake, near the base of the mountain, ninety-eight cabins, Boy Scout and Girl Scout camps, a YMCA camp, and other resorts and campgrounds were covered by debris as much as four hundred feet deep. Farther away, people hiking along the Toutle River heard the explosion, looked up,

Dept. of Natural Resources, State of Washington & NOAA

Steam rising from Mt. St. Helens on June 19, 1980. Note the huge crater on the right side of the mountain. A mud flow is visible extending to the right from the cetner.

and witnessed a twenty-to-forty-foot wave of water barreling down the valley. As the river swelled and flooded, it wiped out enormous areas of forest and washed away bridges and roads. Up to eighteen miles from the mountain, more than two hundred houses and cabins were destroyed and many more were left damaged.

Until the eruption of Mount St. Helens, there were only two known casualties from a volcanic natural disaster within the United States—one in Hawaii and one in Alaska. This eruption took the lives of fifty-seven people. Beyond the human toll, Mount St. Helens caused destruction of almost unimaginable proportions. More than two hundred miles of highways, bridges, and railways were destroyed or irreparably damaged. Tens of thousands of prime forest were lost—amounting to more than four billion board feet of saleable timber. And the loss to wildlife was staggering. Nearly seven thousand big game animals (deer, elk, and bear) were killed along with all birds and most small mammals in the area. The state's Depart-

A steam eruption that occurred in early May before the main eruption.

ment of Fisheries estimated that more than twelve million Chinook and Coho salmon fingerlings were killed when hatcheries were destroyed. Additionally, tens of thousands of young salmon died in waters north of the volcano. Farther downwind, beyond the eighteen-mile destruction zone, fine-grained gritty volcanic ash contaminated oil systems and caused short circuits in electrical transformers, which, in turn, resulted in widespread power blackouts. Many agricultural crops, such as wheat, apples, potatoes, and alfalfa were completely destroyed.

And Mount St. Helens wasn't done with its damage on May 18. It continued to erupt and smolder—with two smaller eruptions taking place in late May and mid-April. Total cost of the destruction ranged from $2 to $3 billion. The International Trade Commission estimated that the cost of property damage and cleanup costs alone totaled at least $1.1 billion.

The Disaster Site Today

I performed an analysis of the Mount St. Helens disaster site as part of my responsibility to cover natural disasters for the Appraisal Institute. Having visited the site in 1990, I had the advantage of nearly ten years of observations, statistics, and evaluations to help me.

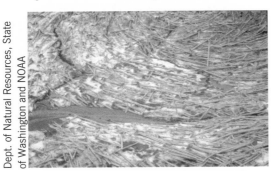

Dept. of Natural Resources, State of Washington and NOAA

Uprooted trees, covered with ash, fill the Green River valley on May 24.

I flew into Yakima and drove the winding mountain roads until I arrived at the national park observatory. To get a more comprehensive view, I climbed to the top of a nearby peak and was absolutely stunned at what I saw. I have been to Hiroshima, the Nevada nuclear test sites, and the Marshall Islands and witnessed the destruction of manmade atomic bombs. But the force of what happened at Mount St. Helens made those nuclear bomb sites look like hiccups. It was the most jaw-dropping site I have ever seen.

As far as the eye could see, mountain over mountain over mountain, all I could observe were knocked over trees. There was not a shred of grass to be seen anywhere. Everything was a stark burnt brown color. It looked like the planet Mars. I just couldn't believe what I was looking at.

With the idea of reaching the summit of Mount St. Helens, I began a hike that I soon regretted. As I moved along, I found myself walking on gray silty ash and stepping over downed trees of all sizes. I crossed small streams that had nothing whatsoever growing beside them. Occasionally, I passed a car with a burned-out frame.

I've done a lot of mountain hiking, but this particular trek was very different from any I had previously been on. The sense of scale was unusually deceptive. I walked three or four hours and ended up nowhere near where I thought I'd be. There was no shade because there were no living trees anywhere. I was just pounded by the sun. Knowing that I would never make it to the rim of the volcano, I finally gave up and turned back. It was the very first time I had ever given up on a hike. But I had to. It was just taking too much out of me.

Today, the destruction caused by the eruption of Mount St. Helens can be categorized into three zones. The Direct Blast Zone averaged about twelve miles in radius from the volcano's peak. Virtually everything, natural or manmade, was obliterated or carried away. Some also called this the "tree removal zone" because every tree was completely destroyed or felled. Every property within this zone was also completely destroyed—including the Boy and Girl Scout camps, the YMCA camp, and all the resorts around Spirit Lake. The lake itself is still there—but smaller and with a different configuration.

The Channelized Blast Zone extended as far as eighteen miles from the volcano. The flow of volcanic material and debris was channeled to some extent by topography—surging through valleys and other low areas. In this zone, nearly everything was destroyed. A few remaining structures still stand near the outer edges, but they are unrepairable and uninhabitable.

Finally, the Seared Zone is the outermost fringe of the impacted area. In this zone, trees remained standing but were singed brown by the hot gasses of the blast. Gray volcanic ash also coated the landscape up to several feet in depth.

Not long after the eruption, the United States government set aside about 110,000 acres for the Mount St. Helens Volcanic Monument. It is now one of the leading tourist attractions in the state of Washington. At the observatory near the summit, there is a playground with a small volcano (kind of like a jungle gym) that the kids can climb on.

As the years have gone by, much of the area has begun to green up. The remarkable perseverance of Mother Nature has gradually vegetated much of the land and most of the wildlife have returned. But the landscape is still a stark, unattractive place—a living monument to the awesome force of one of the most destructive volcanic blasts in human history.

Impact and Insight

The eruption of Mount St. Helens resulted in destruction across more than 150,000 square miles. And its impact on real estate varied widely. In general, the closer to the volcano itself, the greater the impact.

Within the area of the Direct Blast Zone, which was largely a fan-shaped area to the north of the mountain peak, there is currently no value—zero dollars. Virtually everything from the eruption to Spirit Lake was completely destroyed. There is no infrastructure left. It is essentially a vast wasteland, a desert. Property values in this area will not rebound anytime soon.

Interestingly enough, on a novelty basis, some people have purchased small bits of property for $500 or $750 just to be able to say they owned part of the Mount St. Helens destructive zone. This is a very unusual circumstance in terms of real estate impact and values. As a matter of fact, I've never before seen it occur. It is equivalent, I believe, to owning some property on the moon. The real, common sense value of the property, however, is still zero.

In the Channelized Blast Zone, areas farthest from the volcanic peak have seen some land banking or land speculating. Developers have purchased land with the hope that in twenty years the area will come alive. The purchase prices, however, have been very low.

Flooding destroyed many of the areas down river. In some places, the course of the river was actually altered. Other areas experienced complete alteration of elevations over thousands of acres. These changes in topography created a nightmare for land surveyors. Not only were they unable to work with the original elevation, they had no existing landmarks from which to gauge perspective. As a result, landowners were not certain what land they really owned.

Another interesting impact was the damage caused by flooding. While many homes were completely wiped out, others were covered in silt six feet deep. But property owners learned, to their dismay, that their basic insurance policy did not cover flood damage. Nor did it cover the loss of the land—only the structure. Some property owners were eventually reimbursed by the United States government, which condemned their properties and paid them fair market value. But

not everyone received this remuneration. For many, the losses suffered were total—and devastating.

Within the Seared Zone and more peripheral areas, there was not a great deal of damage. For those areas that are buildable, there is no measurable market resistance over the fear of another eruption. This area has really developed at quite a normal pace. Some agricultural areas actually benefited from the volcanic ash that added nutrients to the soil.

Tourism has also been positively impacted. While the initial public reaction to the May 18 eruption dealt a crippling blow to tourist activity, the negative impact proved only temporary. After everything settled down and a road was built up to the observatory, people flocked to view the destruction first hand. In the long run, therefore, portions of the area's economy actually may have been boosted as a result of the eruption.

Lessons Learned

1. Trust Scientists and Their Data

In 1975, geologists published a report predicting that Mount St. Helens was the volcano in the lower forty-eight states most likely to erupt by the end of the twentieth century. Five years later, it happened.

The scientists were not only correct long term, but they were correct short term. In the months preceding the May 18, 1980 eruption, the volcano gave many warning signs—and geologists were on top of all of them. They documented the earthquakes, the localized steam blasts and explosions, and measured "The Bulge" as it grew. Then they issued dramatic warnings to local government agencies.

The Mount St. Helens natural disaster is a prime example of scientists making a huge difference. If it hadn't been for the geologists and their data, there is no doubt that hun-

dreds, perhaps thousands, of lives would have been lost when the volcano blew.

2. Heed Government Warnings about Looming Natural Disasters

As with many natural disasters, numerous official warnings were issued by various government agencies. Unfortunately, most of the people killed in the Mount St. Helens volcanic eruption simply ignored the admonitions to stay out of what was then called the twenty-mile "Red Zone." Some residents even forced their way past police roadblocks and barriers to get to their properties.

One man who lived on Spirit Lake, Harry Truman, even became a local folk hero for refusing to heed repeated warnings and leave his home. Tragically, Mr. Truman and other people with an "It-can't-happen-to-me" mindset are now buried under four hundred feet of volcanic ash.

This photo was taken on May 19, 1983, three years after the explosion. It shows steam releasing from a growing lava dome inside the explosion crater.

University of Colorado and NOAA

7

Auschwitz Concentration Camp

Oswiecim, Poland
June 1940–January 1945

The Disaster

At the beginning of World War II, Nazi Germany enacted laws that deprived Jewish citizens of their basic civil rights. All across Nazi-occupied Europe, Jews were isolated in ghettoes where they suffered from hunger, epidemics, and execution by Nazi death squads. These ghettoes were subsequently liquidated as millions of Jews were deported to various concentration camps where they were to be, as Adolph Hitler dictated, "exterminated without exception." Auschwitz was the largest and harshest of these death camps.

Situated near the small town of Oswiecim, Poland (about forty miles west of Krakow), Auschwitz was originally an abandoned Polish military camp adapted by the Nazis to imprison ten thousand people. There were three main reasons this site was chosen. First, it was centrally located amid the German-occupied countries of Poland, Austria, and Czechoslovakia. Second, there were convenient railway connections nearby. And third, the desolateness of the area ensured that it would be sufficiently isolated from the outside world.

The first prisoners were brought to Auschwitz in June 1940 and full capacity was reached by March 1941. At that time, an additional camp (large enough to confine 100,000 people) was ordered built. That camp, now known as Auschwitz II or

Birkenau, was located a little less than two miles from Auschwitz I. With time, another forty-six forced-labor "sub-camps" were constructed in the surrounding area.

The Auschwitz facilities took up approximately five hundred acres. Sharp barbed-wire fences and a series of guard posts enclosed them. Beyond that, the Nazis constructed a ring of canals more than eight miles long. The entire system was guarded by anywhere from 2,500 to 6,000 callous and often sadistic Nazi SS soldiers. Escape from this concentration camp was virtually impossible.

A large sign over the camp's entrance read: "Arbeit Macht Frei" ("Work Makes You Free"). It was part of an outward-appearing design to give the impression that the purpose of Auschwitz was to train people in "the Nazi way of life." In reality, however, Auschwitz reflected the Nazi policy of "Extermination Through Work"—and quickly escalated into Hitler's main operational facility for the systematic mass extermination of the Jewish people.

Just about everything in the camp was geared toward death. There were beatings, hangings, executions by firing squads at the "wall of death," deliberate malnutrition, and most infamously, mass murder by poison gas. After an experimental gassing (using Cyclon B poisonous gas) of 600 malnourished and ill Russian prison-

The Front Gate at Auschwitz.

ers, numerous gas chambers were constructed by engineers and managers from German industrial companies. Many of the gas

chambers were built to resemble shower rooms that could kill six thousand people each day. Crematoriums were also constructed to dispose of the dead bodies. By mid-1942, murder was occurring on an industrial scale. And by July 1944, it is estimated that more than one million people had been "exterminated" at Auschwitz—ninety percent of them Jewish.

At the height of Auschwitz operations, special trains arrived every day. Each train contained thousands of Jews brought from the evacuated ghettoes in Europe. Each car was filled with people who had been crammed in standing up. They came from Belgium, Greece, Hungary, Holland, and Poland—from Czechoslovakia, Austria, Slovakia, Yugoslavia, and France. Upon arrival, the trains pulled up next to a special ramp. This platform became what many have called the busiest railway station in all of Europe. But it was a one-way station only. The arriving trains were always full. The departing trains were always empty.

The Jews were hurriedly forced out of the train cars and

made to leave their belongings behind. They were told that they were going to be sent to work but would first have to shower and undergo disinfection. Males and females were immediately separated into two lines and directed toward Nazi

Prisoners being taken off the cattle cars at the Auschwitz-Birkenau rail yard ramp. This photo was taken in 1944 by the SS.

SS officers who made a very quick selection process. Some of those who were fit to work were moved to the right. People who were disabled, sick, elderly, or otherwise determined not to be able to perform physical labor were sent to the left—as were all children. When mothers refused to be separated from their children, they were either shot on the spot or simply allowed to go to the left. What they did not know was that to be ordered to the left meant immediate death. These were the people who would go directly to the gas chambers. Seventy-five to eighty percent of all Jews who arrived at Auschwitz were immediately motioned to move to the left.

The Nazis' plan was to kill as many as possible before the next train arrived. Victims were made to undress and then stuffed into the gas chambers as tightly as possible—sometimes as many as two thousand at a time. It was pitch dark inside. The doors were locked shut and the gas was sent in. After fifteen minutes, corpses were then put into the crematoria and burned. Each oven had doors on both sides. The bodies were put in on one side and the ashes were shoveled out from the other side, put into wheelbarrows, and then dumped into a vast pond.

Crematorium ovens in Auschwitz I Museum.

This process went on all day and all night for years. The air for five miles around was filled with choking smoke and ash from the cremated bodies. At the height of the process, it is estimated that between 20,000 and 25,000 people were killed in an average twenty-four-hour period.

People who did not go directly to the gas chambers had their heads shaved, numbers tattooed on their arms, and were given gray and white striped prisoner uniforms. It is estimated that, over the course of five years, more than 400,000 prisoners were registered in this manner at Auschwitz.

Most of these people had to perform forced labor. Some would clean out the train cars, then sift and separate the dead's belongings for things of value. Some would pull gold from the teeth of the corpses—gold that the Nazis would later melt down and use to fund the war. Others were forced to participate in various aspects of the killing—such as putting the bodies into the crematoria or shoveling out the ashes. All were subjected to hunger and malnutrition—or to the torture of sadistic Nazi SS officers. If they complained, they were shot, hanged, or beaten to death with wooden clubs. If they became sick or were in any way unable to work, they were immediately sent off to the gas chambers. It was a bone-chilling, inhumane existence.

And then there were the so-called "medical experiments," the most heinous of which were performed by Dr. Josef Mengele in Block 10 of Auschwitz I. The "Angel of Death," as he was called, was particularly fond of children. He would smile, ask that they call him "Uncle Mengele," and give them candy. Then he would subject them to unbelievable tortures, such as: putting them into pressure chambers; testing them with drugs; injecting chemicals into their eyes in an effort to change their eye color; castrating them; freezing them to death; performing operations on them without anesthesia; and dissecting their dead bodies.

By January 1945, the Soviet army had conducted a major offensive in Poland and was threatening Krakow. Anticipating defeat, the Nazis hastened the killings of those left in the camps by doing such as things as throwing live children into the crematoria and shooting prisoners randomly. They also forced nearly sixty thousand Jews on death marches to remote areas where they were then murdered.

On January 27, 1945, the Soviet army entered Auschwitz. The Nazis had abandoned the camps only hours before after attempting to destroy much of the camp and burn most of the paper documents. The Soviets did, however, liberate more than

This photo, showing guards burning bodies at Auschwitz, was taken by a guard and smuggled out of the camp.

7,600 sick and emaciated people. And, outraged at what they saw, the Russian soldiers destroyed most of the rest of Auschwitz II/Birkenau.

During World War II, more than six million Jews were exterminated by the Nazis in more than a dozen concentration camps scattered strategically across Europe. In five years of existence, no less than 1.5 million Jews were murdered at Auschwitz alone. The place is so infamous that the word "Auschwitz" is now synonymous with the worst evil that humankind can inflict upon itself.

The Disaster Site Today

I traveled to Auschwitz on my way to Chernobyl. I had, of course, heard about the atrocities committed by the Nazis but, as a professional, I was really more interested in seeing what happened to the surrounding real estate. It was only a matter of minutes after I set foot in the death camp, however, that I completely forgot about my profession. Auschwitz was the most heart-wrenching, emotionally devastating place I had ever been to.

After my plane landed in Krakow, I took a train to the small town of Oswiecim. From there, I traveled by automobile the rest of the way. I passed mostly open farmland in what was really quite a beautiful part of Poland. I was enjoying the scenery when the driver suddenly stopped the car and announced that we had arrived. I looked out the window and saw what looked like nothing more than an old industrial building with a brick front.

Photo by Randall Bell

Railroad entrance to Auschwitz today.

"We're here?" I asked.

"Auschwitz!" he snapped.

I spent nearly the entire day there—mostly wandering around in disbelief. You can take guided tours, which I did first. But as people are free to roam about on their own, that's how I spent the rest of my day. I was thinking about what the tour guide had said about the death process when I decided to climb up into a guard tower and look around.

That's when it really hit me.

I saw row upon row of concrete slabs that once had barracks sitting on top of them. Even though the Nazis had demolished much of the camp before they left, they could not eradicate the magnitude of the operation. The place was so enormous, so vast, I could not believe it. It simply took my breath away.

When you're standing there looking at it, five hundred acres becomes more than just a number—it becomes land as far as the eye can see. And seeing is believing. Still there is the original double, razor-sharp barbed wire fence surrounding the camp. Still there is the chain of guard posts one kilometer outside the barbed wire. And beyond that is an eight-mile system of deep canals dug by the Nazis. All of this was designed to prevent mass escapes. I could see clearly that, for the victims, there was simply no place to run or hide.

As I walked around inside the death camp, I noticed a kind of military precision, an exactness to everything. I saw it in the train tracks that ended at the long ramps that led to the crematoriums. I saw it in the grove of trees under which women and children huddled with a momentary respite from the snow and rain as they waited their turn to enter the gas chambers.

I descended into the basement where the Nazis began their experiments with cyanide tablets. I walked into the more perfected gas chambers, which were large concrete rooms with double doors on both sides. I could see where the victims were crowded inside through one set of doors—and then carried out through another—straight to the crematoriums. The bodies of the victims were put into the ovens on one side and, on the other, their ashes were taken out, shoveled into wheel-barrows and then dumped into a huge pond. I saw the paths taken by the wheelbarrows. And I saw the pond. It is still there.

Also still there is the sign that says "Arbeit Macht Frei"—"Work Makes You Free." I walked under it and then walked into some of the barracks that are still standing. Inside, I could see it was plainly obvious that prisoners were treated like animals and no more. I walked outside and saw the make-shift gallows erected by the Nazis to instantly hang people if something was said or done "wrong." They were right in the middle of the camp for all to see. In a corner of the camp, I stood at the wall where people were executed by firing squads. And I looked out from the bars of the jail cells at that wall—where, as prisoners waited their turn to be shot, they saw others executed. And I walked into Block No. 10 where Dr. Josef Mengele performed his awful "experiments."

It made me ill to realize that this place, this Auschwitz, was just one of many concentration death camps built by the Nazis—Dachau, Bergen-Belsen, Treblinka, Sorbibor, and so many more. I felt ashamed to be a human being. I felt ashamed to be part of a race that could be so evil.

It is very apparent that many people have gone to a great deal of effort to preserve this site for posterity. After the war, some people suggested that the place be torn down—that this shame of humankind be eviscerated from the earth. But on July 2, 1947, the Polish parliament passed a law to forever protect the site of Auschwitz-Birkenau along with all its buildings and installations. It is now considered a monument to humankind's struggle against evil. And for Jews the world over, it is a symbol of the holocaust—an event that must never be forgotten so that it never, ever happens again.

Today, Auschwitz is a preserved site protected by the Pol-ish Ministry of Culture and Art. It is a formal state museum dedicated to preservation, research, and education. Many of the exhibits were found on the site during excavations. Empty Cyclon B gas cans; prisoner uniforms; suitcases with names and address of the victims; eyeglasses; human hair used to stuff mattresses, and on and on and on.

More than half a million people visit Auschwitz every year. They travel from every continent, every city, every corner of the world. Survivors come to remember. Children come to learn.

And it is a quiet place. Out of respect, people speak only in soft whispered voices. After all, Auschwitz is the largest cemetery in the history of the world.

Impact and Insight

Often I am asked which is the worst disaster I have ever researched. Having studied virtually every major disaster that has occurred in the world, it has always been interesting to me that the world's worst disaster did not involve hurricanes, tornadoes, or volcanoes, but was caused by hatred and religious persecution. Auschwitz is the worst disaster I have ever researched.

The former death camp is today surrounded largely by open countryside that has remained largely unchanged though the decades. Property is inexpensive and occupied by poor farmers who are often seen in the area on horse-drawn carriages that haul hay or fresh vegetables such as turnips and carrots. To me it is something of an irony that life routinely goes on around Auschwitz. My sense is that the poor Polish people who live in the area are aware of the significance of the site, but have the numb feeling that they could not have stopped the Nazis from putting the camp there in the first place.

As Auschwitz is now a museum that is open to the public without charge, normal economics do not play a role. I do not believe this site is ever going to be sold—nor will it ever be destroyed. Furthermore, I believe my profession is inconsequential where Auschwitz is concerned. As it is the epicenter of the world's most horrible tragedy, I sure would never want to try to place a dollar value on it. The site has a priceless place in history. Its lessons invaluable. Its dead to be respected and honored—forever.

Lessons Learned

1. When a Dictator Like Hitler Comes Along, He Should Be Stopped at All Costs

In the years since I visited Auschwitz, the world has witnessed ethnic cleansing in Kosovo and Afghanistan. It has seen the terrorism of Osama Bin Laden, the hatred of the Taliban, and the dictatorship of Saddam Hussein. For people who lived through World War II, all this was like history repeating itself.

Fortunately, Nazi Germany did not have a nuclear bomb. If they had, we can all be certain Hitler would have used it against the world. Hiroshima killed 100,000 people in one moment. Hitler's death camps killed six million Jews over a period of five years.

Auschwitz should remind us all that when a dictator like Hitler comes along, we cannot turn a blind eye. Whoever is in a position to stop such a dictator has a moral obligation to do so.

2. Humanity Has Not Yet Learned the Lesson of Auschwitz

If nothing else, Auschwitz and the Holocaust should have taught us that we must respect people regardless of any ethnic or religious differences. We should have learned that hating and abusing others for no other reason than the fact that they are different from ourselves is simply inept.

Unfortunately, I believe that the lesson drawn from studying Auschwitz is that we, as a human race, have not fully learned our lesson.

Aerial photograph of Auschwitz taken by U.S. Army Air Force on August 25, 1944 and annotated by the CIA.

8

The Good Friday Earthquake
Alaska, U. S. A.
March 27, 1964; 5:36–5:40 PM

The Disaster

On Good Friday 1964 at 5:36 PM, Alaska experienced what is believed by experts to have been the most violent earthquake in the recorded history of the world. Originating at a depth of approximately sixteen miles, the quake's epicenter was located eighty miles east of Anchorage and sixty miles west of Valdez. Its magnitude registered an astounding 9.2 on the Richter Scale and was felt all the way around the world.

The initial shock wave lasted four minutes and included massive vertical and horizontal displacement. Uplift and subsidence occurred over more than 100,000 square miles of Alaska where scientific documentation disclosed that the ground rose and fell as much as thirteen feet. Large cracks opened up in the earth. Glaciers broke into blocks and huge precipices were created. Lateral spreading of the ground resulted in the wholesale devastation of Alaska's transportation infrastructure. Roads and bridges were completely destroyed and the railroad system was terribly damaged. Rails buckled, tracks sheared and separated, trains derailed and railroad trestles crashed to the ground.

Along the coast, a 35,000-square-mile area actually sank a distance of between one and five feet. Enormous sea waves (tsunamis) were generated away from the epicenter and traveled at speeds up to four hundred miles per hour in the open ocean. The earthquake also caused large tidal waves that resulted in some coastal towns being hit with walls of water as high as ninety feet. Thousands of boats and barges were destroyed. And the vast Alaskan fishing industry was virtually wiped out.

Anchorage, Alaska's largest city, was hit hard. Because it straddles a major fault line, deep fissures and crevices developed throughout the metropolitan area. More than half of all waterlines and streets were destroyed. In the downtown section of the city, a full block of 4th Avenue, the main business street, dropped twenty feet so that the second stories of buildings were at street level. More than 150 commercial buildings were subsequently condemned.

Along the coastline near Anchorage, landslides triggered by the earthquake resulted in the massive destruction of residential neighborhoods. Many homes tumbled into the ocean. Others were simply shaken apart. One high-priced subdivision,

U.S. Dept of the Interior and NOAA

This photo was taken at Seward at the north end of Resurrection Bay, after the tsunamis. It shows an overturned ship, demolished Texaco Chemical truck, and the torn-up dock strewn with logs and scrap metal.

Turnagain-By-The-Sea, was completely destroyed by a massive landslide that tumbled many homes into Cook Inlet. After the quake, the neighborhood looked like it had been destroyed by a tornado as more than 215 homes were completely destroyed.

Farther to the west, huge sea waves generated by the quake smashed into Valdez, Alaska. Some broke over the land and sheared off trees a hundred feet above the beach. One actually deposited debris 220 feet above sea level. In the port, a seaman aboard a steamship filmed a cannery sliding into the sea and water pouring like Niagara Falls over a fifty-foot fault scarp. An entire block of ground actually broke off from the land and slid into the water. Much of the town of Valdez was destroyed and almost nothing was left of the waterfront.

The lead point of the vast Alaskan railroad system was located south of Anchorage at the town of Seward. The earthquake destroyed ninety-five percent of that railhead. Boxcars and locomotives were tossed around like toys, nearby oil storage tanks were ignited, and a mile-long stretch of the city collapsed into the sea.

Damage to the railroad facilities at Seward Port.

Because Seward was built at the end of a long narrow inlet to the ocean, it suffered enormous destruction from tidal waves generated by the quake. The inlet acted much like a bathtub that was rocked back and forth. Water sloshed from one side to the other in huge tides. The resulting flooding lasted all night. Numerous oceanfront properties were swept away and many people were either killed or left homeless.

One family watched as the water filled the first floor. They went upstairs to the second floor only to have the water follow them. Then they went out on the roof and watched in horror as the tidal wave knocked the house off its foundation. A father held on tight to his wife and children all night long as the house's roof floated through the trees. Local government officials placed the family on the town's list of presumed dead. But the next morning the waters finally receded and deposited the roof far away from the original home site. The family ultimately walked several miles back into town. But there were

The scarp of the Fourth Ave. landslide, where two and a half blocks of shops, bars, and stores settled until their entrances were below street level.

U.S. Geological Survey, Menlo Park, CA

many similar circumstances across Alaska involving people who were not so fortunate.

Had the disaster not occurred on Good Friday, when many people were at home or at church, many more lives would have been lost. As it was, 130 people were killed and thousands more injured or left homeless. The motion of the earthquake was felt over seven million square miles—nearly the entire state of Alaska. In the first twenty-four hours, eleven aftershocks occurred with a magnitude greater than 6.0 on the Richter Scale. And over the next several weeks, an additional nine aftershocks took place.

During the initial quake, major shaking of land was felt in portions of Western Canada (including the Yukon Territory and British Columbia) and as far south as the state of Washington. The quake also triggered a Pacific-wide tsunami that was the second largest ever recorded. The wave not only devastated towns along the coast of Alaska, it struck with significant force

U.S. Geological Survey, Menlo Park, CA and NOAA

A scar left by the earthquake at the head of the "L" Street landslide is visible through the snow from the lower right corner to the upper left of the photo, passing below several houses.

along parts of the western coast of North America. Serious damages and deaths occurred at Port Alberni, Canada and Crescent City, California. It took five and one-half hours for the tsunami to reach Hilo, Hawaii where minor damage was sustained.

States as far away as Texas and Florida were affected with vertical motions of five to ten centimeters—and small bodies of water sloshed back and forth in Louisiana enough to sink sailboats. There were also oscillations in water wells reported as far away as South Africa. Indeed, seismologists reported that seismic waves traveled around the earth for several weeks after the Good Friday earthquake. Basically, the entire earth vibrated much like a church bell after it had been rung.

The Disaster Site Today

Today, when you travel through Anchorage, you'd never know that it had experienced the most violent earthquake in re-

Photo by Randall Bell

This house was once above sea level. After the Great Alaskan Earthquake, a portion of the continental shelf actually dropped several feet, and now this house is below sea level and periodic tides have destroyed it.

corded history. With one or two exceptions, the city has been almost completely rebuilt. But the disaster is never really out of the minds of residents.

When I visited downtown Anchorage, I walked along 4th Avenue looking for some sort of sign that nearly an entire block had been dropped a full story. But I really didn't notice anything significant. I did visit a small museum that memorializes the earthquake, but I didn't learn anything that I had not already known. It was when a friend of mine took me into a local pub that I started hearing some first-hand accounts. The owner, who had lived in Anchorage his entire life, recounted to me how he and his friends had gone outside during the initial four minutes of the quake and took bets about which side of the street buildings would fall. Nearly everything had to be rebuilt, so they all ended up losing.

Later that same weekend, I drove out and visited the area formerly called Turnagain-By-The-Sea, the high-priced subdivision that was destroyed by a massive landslide. In contrast to downtown Anchorage, none of the destroyed 215 homes were ever rebuilt. But what happened there will never be forgotten. The site is now an area of open space called Earthquake Park. There are monuments, plaques, and walkways through a now heavily wooded, brushy area. If you go off the beaten track and hike through the brush, you'll come to areas that are still opened up with gaping wide holes and cracks that are three to four feet wide and ten feet deep. I climbed into several of them and, believe me, it really gives you a sense of how violent this particular earthquake must have been.

After the earthquake, Valdez, Alaska suffered so much damage that the entire town was moved to a safer locality about four miles away. Nearly every building that wasn't destroyed was eventually lifted, secured, and transported east to the new town site. Today, the new town visitor center offers visitors a walking tour map of the various homes and businesses that were moved from the old town site. You can also visit the original location of Valdez and see what is left of the old pier, streets, and foundations of old shops and houses. Also prominently displayed is a plaque marking the original location of Valdez and the earthquake that struck it.

The moving of an entire town was not isolated to Valdez. It happened in a number of places. The village on Evans Island, Alaska, for instance, was so totally damaged by the earthquake and tidal waves that it was moved to an entirely new island. And downtown Seward, Alaska was also relocated. As a matter of fact, parts of Seward now have a completely new shoreline in many places. While visiting the area, I was amazed to see that many coastal areas near Seward had dropped down so far during the earthquake that they are now actually below water level. The land is simply gone. Nothing can ever be rebuilt on it.

The ocean front properties that were destroyed by tidal waves sloshing back and forth no longer exist. Local officials later determined that it would be simply be too dangerous to rebuild homes there. Part of the site is now a marsh wetland and a large parking lot for recreational vehicles.

In the lower-risk area of this part of the Alaskan coast, a new $60 million ocean research and aquarium facility has been built within the last decade. This new facility is a good example of how the state of Alaska has assessed construction project locations for risk of damage in the event of another catastrophic earthquake.

Impact and Insight

A conventional analysis of the Good Friday Alaskan earthquake's impact on real estate values would be just what you might think. Anchorage, Valdez, Seward, and similar municipalities suffered enormous property losses that will never be recovered. Nothing of substance will ever be built at Turnagin-By-The-Sea or on the original town site of Valdez. A few areas where high-income residential neighborhoods once stood have since been rebuilt—but with low-income, government-subsidized housing. Such occurrences, of course, have resulted in a dramatic drop of raw land values.

Some unconventional impacts on real estate values occurred as a result of this incredibly powerful and disruptive earthquake. For instance, in several places I visited, many houses that were built on the upside stable blocks of major faults did not originally have oceanfront views. Their views were blocked by rows of homes built closer to the water. But during the earthquake, houses built on the downthrown fault blocks were completely destroyed as the land broke off and slid into the sea. That left the houses on the upside land blocks with new oceanfront views—which, in turn, subsequently increased their future sales values.

In all my years of experience, I had never seen anything quite like this. It was as though an act of God had given these property owners something that people, alone, would never have made happen. The unbelievable power of the Good Friday Alaskan earthquake had, quite literally, moved mountains.

Another unconventional impact on real estate values occurred as a result of the "Santa Claus Effect." Prior to Good Friday 1964, the state of Alaska was undergoing some severe economic problems. Unemployment was high, jobs that were available were low paying, and property values, in general, were down. But the earthquake was so devastating that it brought in an unusually high amount of disaster relief funding. In turn, that resulted in an increased number of jobs that had a positive impact on the state's economy.

Disaster relief organizations from all over the world showed up on Alaska's doorstep to help. The U.S. federal government declared much of the state a federal disaster area, which brought in untold amounts of money and provided Alaskan residents and business-owners low-interest loans. Sewers, water systems, electric power plants, railroads, and highway systems were all rebuilt from scratch. It took years for Alaska to recover. But when it did, the state was more economically sound than it had ever been.

Alaskan officials also commissioned geological and engineering studies so that they could learn from the effects of the disaster. They determined, for instance, that structures built on solid rock foundations were damaged far less than those built on unconsolidated soils. The studies also found that the reactions of different types of subsurface materials controlled fracturing, compaction, lurching, and landslides much more significantly than did distance from the epicenter of the quake.

Geologists looking at the big picture were also able to determine that the northwestward motion of the Pacific plate causes the crust of southern Alaska to be compressed and warped as it is forced under the North American Plate. The boundary of these two megaplates is located at the southern coast of Alaska. While the movement of the Pacific plate is only a few meters per year on average, over tens of thousands of years, the compression and stress will cause earthquakes. Therefore, the geologists predicted that earthquakes of this magnitude would most likely occur again and again.

Lessons Learned
1. Study the Disaster in Detail and Apply What You've Learned

After many disasters, people simply do not take time to think about what really happened. As a result, they tend to make the same mistakes over and over again. Following the disastrous San Francisco earthquake of 1906, government officials allowed schools, hospitals, and residences to be rebuilt on active fault lines. In Malibu, California, high waves consistently smash large multimillion dollar homes along the Pacific coast to pieces. And yet, residences are simply rebuilt where they originally stood.

However, the aftermath of the Good Friday Alaska earthquake is a great example of people who vowed to do all they could to minimize the impact of another similar disaster. Geologists and engineers were brought in to take a good hard look at what happened. They conducted extensive studies and the government utilized those studies to take decisive and preventative actions. They marked areas that were prone to damage from a future earthquake—such as, land comprised of loosely consolidated soils, sites likely to incur landslides, and areas where tidal waves were likely to occur. These areas were then designated "nonbuildable."

In addition, building codes were revised to strengthen structures so they could withstand another major earthquake. And because so many cities had no warning of oncoming waves generated from the quake, the state created a new system (the Alaska Tsunami Warning Center) that will quickly warn coastal communities of any future approaching waves. All these preventative measures will not prevent another major earthquake from taking place, but the intelligent actions of Alaskan officials will certainly minimize impacts, damages, and the number of lives lost.

2. After a Terrible Disaster, the Area Affected May Experience a "Santa Claus Effect"

On March 27, 1964, after only four minutes of unbelievable earth trembling and quaking, the state of Alaska encountered entire towns destroyed, utility and transportation infrastructures taken out, homes demolished, and lives lost. Already

suffering from a significant economic recession, Alaskan officials must have been terribly disheartened. They must have felt
that the situation was entirely hopeless.

But people around the world came to their rescue with
such a fervor that desperation was turned into inspiration
and darkness was turned into light. In the aftermath of the
Good Friday earthquake, Alaska experienced a "Santa Claus
effect" where it unexpectedly received gifts to a point where
the state's economic situation was actually transformed from
"recessed" to "thriving."

Such an effect doesn't happen in most disasters. Once in a
while, however, the goodness of the human spirit rises to such
a level that would make even Santa Claus proud.

9

Monsanto Chemical Pollution & Corporate Malfeasance

Anniston, Alabama
1935–2003

The Disaster

Anniston, Alabama is the site of one of the worst environmental pollution disasters in United States history. Contamination is so widespread that long-lasting biotoxins are in the air, in the water, in the ground, and in just about every living thing—including fish, pets, livestock, and locally grown fruits and vegetables. And the levels of dangerous chemicals in the blood of local children and adults are among the highest ever recorded anywhere in the world.

Worse yet, executives for Monsanto Corporation knew about the effects their chemicals had on the environment and human life but chose to continue to produce, dump, and sell the chemicals, anyway. They also concealed their actions from both the government and nearby low-income residents. All this went on for nearly four full decades. And when the proper state and federal authorities finally learned of the extent of the pollution, they, too, kept quiet for more than twenty years. As a result, the people of Anniston suffered numerous health problems, including: skin rashes, cysts, boils, hardening of cardiac arteries, brain tumors, abnormally high rates of cancer, and death.

Before World War II, Anniston was a sleepy little Southern Appalachian town known for its mineral-rich iron works factory. Nestled in the hills of east-central Alabama, it was conveniently located between major railway hubs in Birmingham (sixty miles to the west) and Atlanta (ninety miles to the east). Things began to change in 1935 when Monsanto took over ownership of the seventy-acre Anniston plant complex and started production of the twentieth century "miracle chemical" known as polychlorinated biophenyl (PCB).

Because they conducted heat, but not electricity, PCBs were initially used as insulators in electric transformers and appliances. With time, however, they were made ingredients in an amazing variety of products—caulking compounds, sealants, newsprint, carbon paper, adhesives, deep-fat fryers, bread wrappers, and paint used in water storage tanks and swimming pools (to name a few). Over the next forty years, the production of PCBs (the product was called

Monsanto Plant

Photo by Randall Bell

Aroclors) became a very profitable enterprise, an unusually lucrative source of wealth and jobs. And Monsanto had the market cornered— being virtually the only corporation that produced PCBs in the United States.

Unfortunately, both the World Health Organization and the Environmental Protection Agency would eventually declare PCBs to be cancer-causing carcinogens that, with prolonged exposure, would cause "developmental deficits and neurological problems in children" and increase the risk of almost all major diseases, including heart disease and diabetes. More than sixty years after Monsanto began producing PCBs, one expert would call West Anniston "the most contaminated site in the United States."

It's natural to think that the corporation producing the PCBs really didn't understand the dangers involved. After all, this all started before World War II—back in the days when people didn't really understand that chemical pollution could

Photo by Randall Bell

Monsanto Plant

be dangerous and when there were no strict environmental regulations. The Environmental Protection Agency wasn't even established until 1970.

But in 1937, only two years after Monsanto began producing their product, executives learned that Aroclors were causing factory workers to develop a serious skin rash called "cloracne." Scientific studies further revealed that it caused liver damage in test animals. By the mid to late 1940s, employees of Monsanto customers began suffering from liver damage due to constant exposure to Aroclor fumes. It was then that Monsanto first warned their customers to protect workers.

Despite those warnings, in the 1950s Monsanto customers reported that some worker's wives were developing cloracne by coming into contact with their husband's work clothes. There were even several reported deaths from prolonged exposure to the PCBs. In 1956, alarmed at these early reports, the United States Navy decided to conduct its own safety tests before using Monsanto's product. However, after all test animals were killed in the experiments, the navy refused to use Aroclors. That decision, of course, cost Monsanto a hefty government contract. Afterwards, the company's strategy was to "continue to get information to satisfy ourselves that the use of our fluids is safe

Photo by Randall Bell

under any normal foreseeable conditions" so as to "satisfy nonmilitary customers." Predictably, most Monsanto customers did not take the time (or spend the money) to conduct their own safety tests as did the U. S. Navy.

Deserted Home Near the Monsanto Plant

In the early 1960s, as Monsanto customers began to experience more health problems in their workforces (including the development of hepatitis), Monsanto executives sent out warnings cautioning customers "not to let workers eat lunch in the Aroclor department." Monsanto then began conducting its own studies and found that test animals did not respond well. "The PCBs are exhibiting a greater degree of toxicity than we had anticipated," said one internal memo. Monsanto scientists also tested the local streams and sediment in West Anniston and found "ominous" concentrations of PCBs.

By now, the Anniston plant was "leaking" approximately 50,000 pounds of PCBs per year into Snow Creek and dumping more than a million pounds of waste per year in the local landfills. The company was meeting only minimum regulatory requirements and did not use settling ponds or filters. They simply washed spills into the sewers. When the U. S. Public Health Service inquired about complaints, Monsanto responded by stating that "our experience and the experience of our customers over a period of 25 years have been singularly free of difficulties." The company also did not warn residents of Anniston about toxicity in the local environment. "It is our desire . . ." stated a corporate memo, "not to give any unnecessary information which could very well damage our sales . . ."

By the late 1960s, environmental damage was becoming profound. Company scientists discovered that there was virtually no sign of life in Snow Creek. And

Photo by Randall Bell

Contaminated Creek Near the Monsanto Plant

when they conducted tests by putting fish into the creek, all "turned belly-up and started spurting blood and shedding skin." "It was like dunking the fish in battery acid," said one report.

Monsanto also commissioned the Zoology Department at Mississippi State University to conduct an investigation regarding the "physical, chemical, and biological" properties of the Choccolocco Creek drainage system. The study definitively showed extraordinarily high concentrations of PCBs. As a result, the Mississippi State professors made four recommendations to Monsanto executives:

▶ 1. Do not release untreated waste in the future.
▶ 2. Clean up Snow Creek.
▶ 3. In the event of a future fish kill, collect samples of fish and water and immediately call in a qualified consultant.
▶ 4. A qualified biologist should inspect Choccolocco Creek periodically, perhaps every other month, to document the status quo . . .

Deserted Elementary School Near Monsanto Plant

Photo by Randall Bell

Also in the late sixties, a group of Swedish scientists released studies showing that traces of PCBs could be found throughout the food chain: in fish, birds, even in pine needles. Traces of the chemicals were even found in the hair of Swedish children.

Monsanto executives responded by preparing a media war against what they called "this evil publicity" and then attacked the credibility of the Swedish study. They also formed an internal "Aroclor Ad-hoc Committee" whose mission was to "protect the image of the corporation" in order to "permit continued sales and profits" of $22 million per year. After studying the situation, the committee told corporate executives that "there is little object in going to expensive extremes in limiting discharges." The decision was then made to maintain "one of Monsanto's most profitable franchises" as long as possible. "We can't afford to lose one dollar of business . . ." said one corporate memorandum." "[We should] sell the hell out of them as long as we can," read another.

Rather than following the recommendations of the Mississippi State professors, Monsanto executives decided to conduct more in-house scientific studies. Those results determined that "sediment in the streams miles below our plant may contain up to two percent Aroclor" that "the PCBs are exhibiting a greater degree of toxicity in this chronic study than we had anticipated," and that local livestock (hogs) sampled were highly contaminated with "as much as 19,000 ppm in their fat."

Despite these findings, Monsanto executives did not clean up the streams. They did not cease dumping excess PCBs into the landfills or washing spills into the sewers. They did not warn Anniston residents not to eat livestock. In fact, they said nothing to anybody about what they had learned. Monsanto's Board of Directors did, however, unanimously approve a $2.9 million expansion of PCB operations in its Anniston and Sauget, Illinois plants.

Monsanto's indiscretions began to catch up with them in 1970 when an Anniston city employee discovered that PCB waste material was seeping out of one of its landfills. Three company employees then met with the technical staff director of the Alabama Water Improvement Commission to discuss the problem. For the first time, Monsanto revealed the extent of the pollution in Anniston. Interestingly, the director promised to handle the problem quietly—which meant he would not release any information to the public. He then warned the Monsanto employees not to make any statements that would alert the press. "[If that happens]," he said, "the Alabama Water Improvement Commission would be forced to close Choccolocco Creek and the Martin-Logan Reservoir to commercial and sport fishing."

Meanwhile, the Food and Drug Administration formally contacted Monsanto to inform them that PCBs had been found in milk samples in Georgia. Then the FDA sampled fish in Chocolocco Creek and found the PCB content to be more than fifty times the legal limit. But the FDA did not make their findings public.

Within a year, however, an informed congressional subcommittee released a report heavily critical of Monsanto's pollution practices in Anniston—and the U. S. Justice Department seriously considered filing a lawsuit against the company. Faced with such political pressure—and possibly having to spend as much as one billion dollars in cleanup costs—Monsanto quickly took steps to shift all its PCB production to the Sauget, Illinois plant. And on May 1, 1972—thirty-eight years after it began—all PCB production was ceased in Anniston.

Over the next decade, additional research into the environmental impact of PCBs revealed more dangerous findings.

Cloracne, for example, was found to be still present in some people more than thirty years after they were first exposed. Other studies, conducted by national organizations and in-house Monsanto scientists, revealed that PCBs caused cancer in laboratory animals.

The conclusions of the Monsanto's internal studies were actually altered to lessen the impact of such a negative out-come. The findings of "slightly tumorigenic" were changed to "does not appear to be carcinogenic." The company further issued corporate directives about what to say and do when the subject of PCB carcinogenicity came up. Company spokesmen were told to "avoid" the topic, to "not offer information," to "make no comments," and to use the following statement:

> We have seen nothing in our preliminary health studies with our PCB workers or, indeed, in our extensive long-term feeding studies with animals that would indicate that PCBs are carcinogenic.

In 1993, an employee of the U.S. Soil Conservation Service dis-covered a deformed fish in Chocolocco Creek and sent it off for analysis. When the results revealed extraordinarily high levels of PCBs, the state of Alabama conducted an in-depth investiga-tion that revealed contamination had spread more than forty miles downstream from the Monsanto plant. For the first time, advisories were then issued to local residents not to eat local fish. This was more than twenty-five years after Monsanto con-ducted tests on fish that had turned belly up, spurted blood, and shed skins.

Three years later (1996), comprehensive investigations by the federal government found that PCB levels in Anniston were astronomical:

> ➤ 200 times the federal limit in dust from residential homes;
> ➤ 940 times the federal limit in residential yard soils;
> ➤ 2,000 times the federal limit in Monsanto's drainage ditches.

In addition, nearly a third of Anniston residents living near the Monsanto plant had inordinately high levels of PCBs in their blood streams. These individuals suffered from cancer, learning disabilities, increased rates of asthma, and reproductive deformities. Such revelations, along with other events, spurred the Mars Hill Missionary Baptist Church and more than three thousand residents of West Anniston to file a major lawsuit against Monsanto.

Within a year, Monsanto spun off its chemical operations into a separate company and named it "Solutia." Shortly thereafter, twenty thousand Anniston residents filed five additional lawsuits accusing Monsanto/Solutia of "polluting their community," "threatening their health," "destroying their property," "failing to protect local residents," and "knowingly contaminating Anniston's air, soil, and water with PCBs."

Monsanto/Solutia's defense was that it "didn't know that PCBs were harmful to human health or persistent in the environment until the late 1960s," and "once they were aware of the contamination, they implemented swift and effective plans to stop the releases, repair the damage that had already occurred, and protect the citizens."

However, the Anniston lawsuits discovered the existence of more than a million pages of corporate documents that revealed the weakness of Monsanto/Solutia's defense strategy. Many of the more sensitive memorandums were labeled "C-O-N-F-I-D-E-N-T-I-A-L" with each letter underlined twice— and DESTROY. Thousands of additional documents turned out to be exceedingly damaging to the corporation. As a result, plaintiffs began winning their lawsuits. For example, one jury found Monsanto liable on counts of negligence, nuisance, trespass, wantonness, suppression of the truth, and outrage. "Outrage" meant that the corporate giant was found guilty of engaging in behavior "so outrageous in character and extreme in degree as to go beyond all possible bounds of decency so as to be regarded as atrocious and utterly intolerable in civilized society."

In order to settle all cases, in 2003, Monsanto agreed to pay $600 million in damages to residents and $100 million in cleanup costs and community improvement programs (such as a clinic that provides free health care to local victims). Many local residences and business structures are also being purchased from existing homeowners who live in structures that are too contaminated to be occupied. Some citizens are also calling for the corporation to dredge all the PCBs out of Anniston's streams and creeks. But Monsanto's executives have balked because the cost of such work could easily reach into the billions of dollars.

In response, corporate brochures were handed out to residents of Anniston that read, in part: "Monsanto intends to be a good neighbor."

The Disaster Site Today

Anniston is an easy drive from Birmingham—only about an hour going east on Interstate 20 to Oxford, and then just five minutes north on State Highway 21. It's a little longer, maybe ninety minutes, if you opt to drive down from Atlanta. Either way, you're in for a nice, scenic, leisurely drive.

Upon entering Anniston, however, you begin notice an eerie circumstance. The closer you get to the Monsanto plant, the more you realize that Anniston is half ghost town. All over the place, you see signs of life next to near-utter desolation. I've never really seen anything quite like it. There's an abandoned bank building, unkempt and overgrown with weeds, right next to an active restaurant. There's a small, struggling mom-and-pop market right next to an old abandoned gas station. There's a deserted home right next to an active church. And near the still-active Monsanto plant, there is an abandoned school surrounded by a chain-link fence with barbed wire on the top. The fence reminds you of a prison, but it's obviously there to keep people from entering rather than escaping.

Directly across the four-lane Birmingham Highway (State Road 202), are some scenic, rolling green hills. Actually, as inconspicuous as they are, if you blinked while you were driving by, you would probably miss them. These unassuming hills, however, are the dumps where, for decades, Monsanto deposited its waste and excess PCBs. There is a chain-link fence around the hills, but no warning signs that I could see. And it's believed by many people that the more than five thousand tons of PCBs buried there are still emitting fumes into the atmosphere. One local resident related a story about how his friend had jumped the fence to take a shortcut and, while walking over the "pretty green hills," he burned the soles off his boots.

As you drive through the local neighborhoods in the vicinity of the plant, you see some homes that are occupied and some that aren't. The abandoned houses are all overgrown with vegetation. People who opted to stay behind, though, now have to mow their lawns with masks because the grasses and soils are contaminated. For that reason, also, their children have to play on the sidewalks or in the streets—right next to the trucks that are sometimes scraping the top six inches of soil off the land. Behind one of the neighborhoods runs the still-contaminated Snow Creek. Locals call it "Stink Creek" and tell you horror stories about it—like the puppy that took a sip of water from it and promptly died, or the cancer cluster in homes right beside it.

Even though Snow Creek and these communities were declared public health hazards, I saw no warning signs alerting visitors to that fact. Local residents, however, have been told not to kick up dirt, chew gum, eat food, or smoke cigarettes while sitting or standing in their front or back yards. The only signs visitors might see that would alert them that something is out of the norm are small yellow monitors posted in the soil from time to time. These are areas where the PCB concentration is suspected to be unusually high. If you speak with the residents, you learn that many of them suffer from a variety of health problems—including rashes, cysts, boils, hardening of cardiac arteries, brain tumors, and cancer.

Not far from the Monsanto plant is a brand new health center that provides free care to the local victims. And the truth is that many people elected to stick around because they would get free treatment. The plant itself does not have the appearance of something that could have caused so much damage to the environment and human life. It's rather small and almost all of it is painted white. Today, the Monsanto plant is still operating. It manufactures a chemical that is used in Tylenol and executives claim that it has not allowed the release of a toxic material in more than four years. However, if you drive a few miles to the edge of Anniston, you'll see another sign of the times. The United States Army has constructed an incinerator designed to burn several thousand tons of poisonous sarin and mustard gas.

Impact and Insight

The Monsanto disaster's impact on Anniston property values runs a broad spectrum. On one extreme, many homes and businesses have been completely abandoned by their owners.

Today, there is simply no market for the structures left behind. They are totally worthless. On the other extreme, some homes and businesses remain fully functional and continue to appreciate in value. And in the middle, some properties have sold for about fifty percent of their true value. Others have never been sold and, in what is termed "value in use," people continue to live or conduct business on their properties. A "value in use" property does not specifically impact the real estate market.

Clearly, proximity to the Monsanto plant is a factor in determining property values. The closer you get to the plant, the more abandoned homes and buildings you see. The father away, the more things get back to normal. Interestingly, though, there is not necessarily a lower PCB contamination level the farther you get from the plant. Some areas far away are heavily contaminated because the PCBs were transported by water. But because the Monsanto plant is not actually in view, the properties have not suffered much diminution in value. This situation is more one of perception than anything else. It's an "out of sight, out of mind" mentality.

True market value is reflective of a sale or of a hypothetical sale—where both the buyer and the seller are informed of all pertinent information regarding all aspects of the property. But in an area where business and industry are concealing information about surface contamination, you may not see a measurable impact on property values. Whereas if they were informed, you may see an impact. When the buyer and the seller are uninformed, it's very possible that some properties will sell at full value.

PCBs are invisible. Like radioactivity, you really cannot know how bad the contamination is unless you monitor things on a regular basis. And how long do they remain in the soil? According to the latest scientific studies, PCBs remain in the soil for *at least* a century. Therefore, there really isn't much of a future for any kind of development (residential or business) in the immediate vicinity of the Monsanto plant.

Lessons Learned

1. Some People Will Do Anything for Money

With PCB production, corporate executives at Monsanto knew they had a big moneymaker. And they went to extraordinary lengths to keep the public in the dark about the harmful effects of their product. They not only ignored mainstream scientific findings, they ignored their own studies and changed conclusions so as to lesson the impact on public opinion and knowledge. In effect, Monsanto's corporate culture included a concerted effort to deceive the public.

In addition, this disaster demonstrates a failure of government to protect its citizens—on the local level, the county level, the state level, and the federal level. Normally, at one of those points, somebody picks up the information and raises a red flag. But in this case, nobody put a stop to it. And it went on for generations.

Clearly, there is a strong indication of government corruption in this case. Monsanto's business was such an enormous moneymaker, no one was about to rock the boat. And when the situation is viewed in strict economic terms, Monsanto made an "acceptable" decision. In relation to the money that was made over six decades, a $700 million settlement was relatively inconsequential.

What does all this tell us? What is to be learned from the Monsanto disaster?

Well, it demonstrates to us that there is a segment of our society that has a wanton disregard for other people. As a matter of fact, it has a wanton disregard for anything but the almighty buck. For these corporate executives and their PCB cash cow, people getting sick just didn't enter into the equation.

2. The Bad Guys Don't Always Get What They Deserve

In civil court, Monsanto was found to have engaged in activity "so outrageous in character and extreme in degree as to go beyond all possible bounds of decency so as to be regarded as atrocious and utterly intolerable in civilized society." And yet, executives for the corporation were totally unapologetic for their actions. Not only did they admit no wrongdoing, they repeatedly asserted that they had "nothing to be ashamed of."

When one former manager was asked if Monsanto officials had ever shared their findings about PCB hazards in Anniston with members of the community, his response was: "Why would they?" Other executives stated that Monsanto was "really proud of what we did," and that "we mostly did what any company would do, even today." These people did not act like good corporate citizens. They didn't even act like decent human beings. No criminal charges were ever filed. Why not?

This story is like a movie without a happy ending. The ending, rather, is tragic. The bad guys did not get what they deserved. They're not in jail. They're still walking the streets. And they are all rich. Sometimes, life isn't fair—and you just have to learn to live with it. Justice will have to come in another lifetime.

10

Terrorist Attacks

World Trade Center, New York City
Pentagon, Arlington, VA Shanksville, PA
September 11, 2001

The Disaster

It was the deadliest act of domestic terrorism in the history of
the United States. Every American remembers where they
were when they heard the news. Millions witnessed the events
live on television. Four major airliners were converted into flying bombs. The entire World Trade Center and part of the Pentagon were destroyed. It cost tens of billions of dollars in
cleanup and rebuilding costs. $40 billion was paid out by insur-
ance companies. It resulted in an estimated economic loss of
more than $100 billion. A total of 3,209 innocent people were
killed. And the United States went to war because of it.

September 11, 2001 began normally enough. It was Tues-
day morning, the second day of the business week. People had
just awakened, were having breakfast, or were headed to
work. Across the Eastern seaboard, the weather was bright,
sunny, and clear. In the Washington, D.C. area, the sun rose
into a crisp, cloudless sky. In New York City, the Hudson Bay
was calm, the water like glass. And in Massachusetts, the
morning brought a cool autumn breeze and the promise of
another pretty New England day.

But all that began to change when two major airliners left
Boston's Logan Airport bound for Los Angeles. American Air-

www.bigfoto.com

lines Flight 11, a Boeing 767 with eighty-one passengers and eleven crewmembers, took off at 7:50 AM (fourteen minutes after its scheduled departure). And United Airlines Flight 175, also a Boeing 767, took off sixteen minutes late (at 8:14 AM) carrying fifty-six passengers and a crew of nine. Everything seemed routine.

About fifteen minutes into American Flight 11, five men tied red bandannas around their heads and, armed with box cutters and knives, stormed the front of the plane. One of the hijackers had a box with yellow wires attached to his waist and claimed it was a bomb. When two first-class flight attendants and a passenger confronted them, they were stabbed and thrown aside. Once they quickly gained access to the cockpit, they directed the pilot to turn off the plane's transponder. He did as ordered but also quietly activated the talk-back button, which enabled Boston flight controllers to hear what was going on.

Right about this time, at 8:20 AM, ten minutes after its scheduled departure, American Airlines Flight 77, a Boeing 757, left Dulles International Airport near Washington, D.C. There were fifty-eight passengers and six crewmembers on board. The plane headed due west toward Los Angeles, its planned destination.

Back on American Flight 11, two flight attendants, Amy Sweeney and Betty Org, made separate cell phone calls. "Listen to me and listen carefully," one said, "I'm on Flight 11. The airplane has been hijacked. The hijackers are of Middle Eastern descent." The women went on to report that two flight attendants had been stabbed and a passenger's throat had been slashed. They were dying. The hijackers had also sprayed something in the first-class cabin to keep people out of the front of the plane. It burned the women's eyes and they were having trouble breathing. They were providing oxygen to the injured people and had asked if there was a doctor on board.

Around 8:30 AM, pilot was apparently pulled from his seat. Soon thereafter, transmissions on the talk-back button ceased. Over Albany, the plane made an unplanned 100-degree turn to the south. Betty Org reported that the plane tilted all the way on one side and then became horizontal again. Amy Sweeney stated that they were now descending rapidly. One of the hijackers got on the public address system. "Nobody move, please," he said. "We are going back to the airport. Don't try to make any stupid moves." The plane was now headed on a straight-line path to New York City.

At 8:40 AM, flight controllers asked the pilots aboard United Flight 175 to look for a lost American Airlines plane ten miles to the south. They responded that they had, indeed, made visual contact with the plane and that they had heard a suspicious transmission shortly after take off from Boston. Flight controllers then instructed the pilots to stay away from Flight 11.

At Newark International Airport, United Airlines Flight 93 finally took off for San Francisco at 8:42 AM. It had been scheduled to leave at 8:01 AM but was delayed due to heavy runway traffic. It was a Boeing 757 with thirty-eight passengers and seven crewmembers on board. The plane headed due west across New Jersey and Pennsylvania.

At virtually the same moment United 93 took off, five hijackers on United 175 stormed the front of the plane. One of the passengers, Peter Hanson, called his father. "Oh, my God!"

DoD photo by Tech. Sgt. Cedric H. Rudisill

FBI agents, fire fighters, rescue workers and engineers work at the Pentagon crash site on Sept. 14, 2001.

he said. "The plane is being hijacked. They're stabbing the flight attendants to force the crew to unlock the doors to the cockpit." Shortly thereafter, a nearby plane picked up an emergency locator transmitter (ELT) signal from Fight 175.

At 8:45 AM, Amy Sweeney was still on the phone aboard American Flight 11. She was asked if she could look out the window and recognize where she was. "I see the water," she responded. "I see the buildings. Oh, my God!" Betty Org, on another line, began repeating the phrase, "Pray for us. Pray for us. Pray for us." A moment later, American Flight 11, traveling at 470 miles per hour and carrying ten thousand gallons of jet fuel, crashed into the north tower of the World Trade Center. It tore a gaping hole in the side of the building and exploded in a massive fireball.

Just as American Flight 11 crashed into the World Trade Center, United 175's transponder signal was turned off. The plane, which had just entered New Jersey, then made a major turn and headed directly to New York City. An unidentified flight attendant on board called the airline maintenance center in San Francisco. "Oh, my God!" she said. "The crew has been killed, a flight attendant has been stabbed. We've been hijacked!" Then the line went dead.

A minute later, American Flight 77 out of Dulles International went severely off course. Just as it crossed into West Virginia, it turned due north for a while, then south, then back to the west again. Flight controllers reported that the pilot was not responding to routine instructions and that the plane's transponder signal had been turned off.

Back on United Flight 175, at 8:58 AM, passenger Brian Sweeney, called his wife and mother. "We've been hijacked and it doesn't look too good." Peter Hanson called his father again and said goodbye. Seconds later the plane crashed into the south tower of the World Trade Center and exploded into another massive fireball.

Millions of people witnessed this event live on television. News reporters noted that as many as fifty thousand people worked in the World Trade Center Towers on a normal business day.

Both towers were now burning. Smoke was billowing out everywhere. Glass, steel beams, millions of pieces of paper, body parts, and other debris flew out of the buildings and littered the streets below. Emergency alarms sounded all across the city. Fire trucks, ambulances, police cars, and other emergency vehicles rushed to the scene. And while thousands of people poured out of both towers, hundreds of New York firefighters and policemen charged in.

At 9:25 AM, a passenger on American Flight 77, Barbara Olson, called her husband in Washington, D.C. She said the plane had been hijacked shortly after takeoff. The hijackers were armed with box cutters and knives and all the passengers had been herded to the back of the plane. About this time, the Federal Aviation Administration observed that just before Flight 77 reached West Virginia's border with Kentucky, it turned 180 degrees and headed back toward Washington, D.C.

Also at 9:25 AM, the pilot on United Flight 93 performed a routine check in with air traffic controllers in Cleveland. A minute or two later, a group of hijackers with red bandanas around their heads stood up and yelled something. One had a small red box strapped to his waist. He grabbed the public address microphone and, with a Middle Eastern accent, announced that he was the pilot, that there was a bomb onboard, and the flight was returning to the airport. Flight controllers heard the sound of screaming and scuffling over an open microphone— and then men speaking in Arabic. The other hijackers stabbed a flight attendant and a passenger. Then they stormed into the cockpit, pulled the pilot and copilot out, slit their throats, and took over the controls of the plane. They turned off the transponder and Flight 93 disappeared from all radar screens. Then the plane reversed course and headed east toward Washington, D.C. It flew along a well-established flight corridor right along the Pennsylvania Turnpike.

First-class passenger Tom Burnett called his wife and told her the plane had been hijacked and that there was a bomb on board. The man sitting next to him had been knifed and was dead. He asked her to call the FBI. When she told him about the other hits on the twin towers, he responded: "Oh, my God! It's a suicide mission."

At 9:35 AM, American Flight 77 crossed the Capitol Beltway and headed directly toward downtown Washington, D.C. Once it reached the Potomac River, the plane made a difficult high-speed descending turn, circled around, and dropped seven

Ground Zero on September 14, 2001.

thousand feet in less than two and one-half minutes. It flew very near the White House, but then turned and headed back across the Potomac. It was now flying at 460 miles per hour and about twenty-five feet off the ground. Its landing gear was up. At 9:43 am, the jet clipped several light poles anchored in a massive parking lot and then crashed into the southwestern side of the Pentagon. A massive fiery explosion resulted and a mushroom cloud ascended skyward.

The Pentagon is the main headquarters of the United States military. More than twenty thousand people work in the building on a normal business day.

The White House and the U. S. Capitol building, believed by federal authorities to be likely targets, were immediately evacuated. The Federal Aviation Administration then halted all flight operations at all airports across country. It was the first time such an action had been taken in United States history. All

Ground Zero on September 18, 2001

Photo by Randall Bell

Photo by Randall Bell

Ground zero on September 18, 2001.

planes in the air were ordered to land at the nearest airport. Once an inventory was completed, the FAA sent out an alert. There was one plane unaccounted for and it was flying on a direct path to Washington, D.C.

Back on United Flight 93, a number of other passengers were making phone calls. Jeremy Glick called his wife. Marion Britton called a friend. Sandra Bradshaw and Cee Cee Lyles called their husbands. Mark Bingham and Elizabeth Wainio called their mothers. Todd Beamer spoke to a telephone operator.

The passengers had been split into two groups. One group was in first class being guarded by the hijacker with the bomb. The other was huddled in the rear of the plane. One passenger was definitely dead. The two pilots were apparently dead. They all learned that the Pentagon had been hit. They all passed on messages to their families that they loved them.

Tom Burnett was in first class. He explained to his wife that the hijackers were talking about crashing the plane into the ground—and that he believed the bomb was a fake. He said that he and the others were making a plan to take back the plane over a rural area. "We're going to do something about this."

Jeremy Glick said that the passengers in his group had taken a vote to determine if they should try to take back the plane or not. They vote was "yes."

At 9:57 AM, they were ready to make their move. Sandra Bradshaw and the other flight attendants filled pitchers with hot water to throw on the hijackers. Tom Burnett said: "I think we can do it!" Mark Bingham and Jeremy Glick yelled: "Let's get them!" Todd Beamer said, "Are you guys ready? Okay, let's roll!"

The passengers then stormed the front of the plane. There was screaming and fighting in the first class cabin. "They're doing it!" someone yelled. "They're doing it!" The two hijackers in the cabin were quickly overpowered.

"In the cockpit!" someone was heard to yell. "Let's get them! In the cockpit!"

They passengers used a food cart as a battering ram to break down the door—the sound of plates and glassware clanging could be heard. One of the hijackers in the cockpit asked, "Should we finish?" The other responded, "Not yet!" Then they begin chanting: "Allah o akbar! God is great!"

The door finally gave way and several passengers made it into the cockpit. Some fought the hijackers while others grabbed the controls.

"I'm injured," someone screamed.

"Lift it up!" said another. "Pull it up."

In Lower Manhattan at the World Trade Center, things were getting desperate. Thousands of people were still evacuating the buildings. Dozens trapped on the upper floors were leaping from the windows and falling to their deaths.

Suddenly, a thunderous quaking rumble began. It sounded like a freight train coming. The south tower was collapsing to the ground. A massive cloud of cement dust, steel girders, and other debris filled the air. It looked like ash from an erupting volcano. The top floor hit the ground in less than ten seconds. Thousand of terrified people on the ground ran for their lives. They headed down streets, alleyways, and into buildings. Some scrambled under cars. There was screaming, wailing, and mass confusion.

Now over a lightly populated part of Somerset County, Pennsylvania, United Flight 93 rocked back and forth several times as the passengers fought the hijackers for control. The plane was flying low to the ground and moving very fast. It banked to the right and appeared to be trying to climb high enough to clear a ridge. But it started to spiral and then turned upside down. Suddenly, it made a downward turn of nearly ninety degrees and nosedived into the ground. The impact resulted in a thunderous explosion and an enormous mushroom cloud.

United Flight 93 crashed at 10:06 AM in an isolated field near Shanksville, Pennsylvania—more than a hundred miles short of the terrorists' destination in Washington, D.C. There were no survivors.

Twenty minutes later, the remaining World Trade Center tower collapsed onto itself from the top down—the floors above slamming onto each successive floor below until the structure disappeared into another enormous cloud of debris, dust, and smoke. Lower Manhattan now looked like a devastated European war zone of World War II. New York City Mayor Rudolph Giuliani ordered an evacuation of Lower Manhattan. When asked about the number of people killed, he responded: "I don't think we want to speculate about that. It may be more than any of us can bear."

The Disaster Sites Today

Normally, a good period of time goes by before I visit a disaster site. In this case, however, I was there less than a week after it happened—when things were still smoldering. I had been due to make a presentation in New York the week after

September 11. Naturally, I presumed the event would be canceled, but my clients called and asked me to make the trip. "Randy, we are so stunned here, that we really want to have an event to get everybody together," they explained. "We'd like a little bit of normality restored to our lives. But if you don't want come, we certainly understand."

I flew from Los Angeles to Newark on American Airlines. Both airports were like church on Mondays—nobody was there and it was unbelievably quiet. There were also only about three or four people on the entire plane. I was sitting on the left side as we approached New York. It was at night and there were huge floodlights illuminating the site. When I saw Ground Zero, my heart almost stopped. No more twin towers. A war zone of destruction. Smoke still billowing from the rubble. It was awful.

The next day, after my presentation, I went down to Ground Zero. The disaster was on such a scale that there is no picture that really shows the reality of the situation. The debris was ten stories high—taller than most high rise buildings. And the smell was indescribable and overwhelming. Fires were still smoldering. At one point, I was walking down the street and a manhole cover that I had just walked over popped out and flames shot out of the hole. Then a fireman said to me: "Hey, you really need to get out of here." In that moment, the dangers experienced by the firemen and relief workers really came home to me.

People in New York were simply stunned. The normal hustle and bustle wasn't there. Everybody was being very cordial and respectful toward each other—and unusually quiet. Buddhist monks gathered on the sidewalks to offer prayers. And Lower Manhattan was plastered with pictures and cards that said things like: "Have you seen my son, or daughter, or father or mother, or husband or wife." They were everywhere.

Fires at Ground Zero continued to burn for three months while rescue workers removed and sifted through the debris. In addition to the twin towers, five other buildings in the World Trade Center complex were destroyed or partially damaged—and more than twenty other structures in the immediate vicinity underwent significant repairs or rebuilding. Rescue and recovery took eight months—and was completed at the end of May 2002.

The Pentagon was rebuilt within a year. People worked day and night in rescue, recovery, and rebuilding. Today the building looks virtually the same as it did on September 10, 2001. The government's attitude in moving with speed was straightforward: "We are going to send the terrorists a message. The United States of America is resilient and will not be kept down."

The little town of Shanksville is five minutes off the Pennsylvania Turnpike. If you turn north at the red light (Lambertsville Road) and go one mile, you'll hit Buckstown Road. Take a right and go another mile and you'll come to an obscure country road. A left hand turn and another few hundred yards will be the site where United Flight 93 crashed.

For two weeks following September 11, this rural area was a federal crime scene. The crash blew a forty-foot crater in the landscape. Witnesses said that, unless you had seen the plane go down, you'd never know what happened. There were no large remnants, no large chunks of fuselage. Most of the material recovered was no bigger than a dinner plate. Basically, there was just a big smoking hole in the ground. A zone of small debris also extended half a mile across a field, through a tree line, and onto a couple of barns and cabins. Fortunately, the area was in such a remote part of Pennsylvania that no one on the ground was injured.

Today, two chain-link fences encircle the 128-acre site. An inner fence surrounds the impact crater. This is referred to as "the hallowed ground" and is treated as reverently as a cemetery. No one is allowed to walk inside and officers from the local sheriff's office regularly guard it. A second fence circles the perimeter of the entire area. Both fences are six feet high. In between them is open green space.

At the end of the small country road, on an elevated piece of land, is a temporary memorial to the passengers and crew of Flight 93. Near the outer fence are flowers and wreaths, various plaques, religious symbols, letters, notes, pictures, numerous American flags of all sizes, and yellow ribbons tied around trees. Many of these tokens have been left behind by people who have come from all around the world to pay their respects. An average of five thousand people visit the site each week—day and night, rain or shine. And volunteers from the local community are usually on hand to make presentations, provide a historic overview, and answer questions.

Impact and Insight

Within half an hour after Flight 175 crashed into the north tower of the World Trade Center, I received a long distance call from a reporter for the London Times. She asked me what I thought this disaster would mean in terms of real estate. My immediate response was that it might result in the corporate world's love affair with high-rise offices building being less desirable in the future.

A couple of days later, representatives of several other agencies asked me if I thought property values would go down and if the World Trade Center site would ever be rebuilt upon. While I was aware that there would be a huge emotional factor attached to the tragedy, I also knew that, economically, the site had to be rebuilt. "There will not be a long term impact on property values," I told them. "The site will be rebuilt but will most certainly include a memorial to the people who lost their lives."

In the aftermath of September 11, there were two major factors that had real potential to impact long-term real estate values in the New York area. In the end, neither came into play. First, there was the very real concern that mass quantities of residents were simply going to put their properties up for sale and move away. After all, this was the second major terrorist attack on New York City. Such an event, with so many residences up for sale, would surely have dropped property values. And, in truth, many people were fed up and did want to leave. But after taking time to think about it, most people stayed put. They did not want the terrorists to win. Mass quantities of people fleeing New York would have given them a victory.

The second factor revolved around the reality that approximately 12.5 million square feet of class A office space had been completely destroyed—and an additional 13.3 million were damaged. Many corporations, government agencies, and private businesses were forced to relocate. There was no other

Photo by Randall Bell

Flight 93 Memorial Site near Shanksville, Pennsylvania.

option. Vacant office space in New York quickly filled up. There was also a major spillover effect in the New Jersey market. As a matter of fact, an earlier belief that New Jersey office space wasn't as desirable as office space in New York quickly went away. Now, here we have a simple case of supply and demand. Prices should have risen significantly. But neither the cost of office space rentals nor property values went up. Prices were deliberately restrained out of respect. People did not want to capitalize on a tragedy like this. There was no price gouging—and organizations ended up moving into new office space for the same prices that existed before September 11.

There were also a variety of factors that occurred in the aftermath of September 11 that could have impacted real estate values, but did not. For instance, more than 140,000 jobs were lost in New York. Economic loss to the city in the months following the attacks amounted to $105 billion. The estimated cost of the cleanup was $600 million. $7.5 billion had to be spent overhauling the subways in Lower Manhattan. And insurance claims amounted to more than $40 billion.

Despite all these factors, real estate values in Lower Manhattan were not significantly impacted. Of course, someone could make the case that since there were no longer buildings there, the values had to go down. And in the short-term market, I suppose that's a valid point. But in the long term, real estate values did not go down. On balance, they pretty much stayed the same and continued on a normal cycle. Real estate in Lower Manhattan averaged $5 million an acre on September 10, 2001 and two years later, it averaged $5.1 million per acre. The difference is negligible. Moreover, the mere fact that the property was originally so valuable had an enormous influence on what happened in the aftermath of September 11. It was worth too much to go down—and it was so high, there was no room to go up. So it pretty much stayed the same.

In addition, quickly designed plans for rebuilding on the site ensured that the long-term real estate market would be healthy and vibrant. The new World Trade Center site will include large, very nice office buildings. Square footage will be comparable to the twin towers complex. But rather than two very tall dominating building, there will be four or more of lesser heights. The tallest will be called "Freedom Tower" and will include a spire at the top leading to the symbolic height of 1,776 feet. A tasteful and moving memorial with open green space will be at the center of the new complex. There will be a balance between a memorial and respect for the past while looking at the business of going forward.

There were absolutely no real estate impacts on the Pentagon or the area that surrounds it. Being a huge government building, it is not really exposed to normal markets. And because the Pentagon's complex is situated on approximately six hundred acres, it is well isolated from any other major commercial or residential properties. Damage caused by the tragic crash of American Flight 77 was limited to the grounds of the Pentagon complex.

A memorial is planned on the southwestern side where the plane crashed. It will consist of green space with 184 units being dedicated to all the victims of the tragedy (125 in the Pentagon; 59 in the plane). Each unit will be accompanied by a red-purple broad-leafed tree, a glowing light pool, a cantilevered bench, and a place for the permanent inscription of each victim's name. A sign has already been erected on the site. It reads: "Terrorist attacks can shake the foundations of our biggest buildings, but they cannot touch the foundation of America."

In comparing the New York and Pennsylvania disaster sites in terms of real estate impact, we find two astonishingly opposite situations. In New York, we have some of the priciest real estate in the nation, the Manhattan financial district, which averages $5 million per acre. In Pennsylvania, we have some of the most inexpensive land in the nation—at about $1,000 per acre (before September 11, 2001). There was virtually no impact in New York. But in Pennsylvania, there was a major impact. The value of the land, itself, escalated tremendously. Memorials bring visitors and revenues.

Currently, several hundred thousand people visit the crash site of United Flight 93 each year. With time, that number is likely to increase significantly. The location is only a few miles off a major east-west artery in the northeastern United States—the Pennsylvania Turnpike. Business in the surrounding communities (motels, restaurants, various shops) has already grown significantly and spikes each year on the anniversary of the disaster.

The crash site proper involves one primary and two secondary landowners. Eventual development of an appropriate memorial could involve four or five more. As a result, that land is worth a considerable amount of money in speculation alone. Surrounding areas of potential commercial development will also increase in value.

The aspect of heroism portrayed by the passengers and crew of United Flight 93 is of the highest order. Hundreds, perhaps thousands of people who were in Washington, D.C. owe their lives to the heroes on that airplane. That is both an important and an inspiring story. Some sort of appropriate memorial and museum will be erected on the site. And many people believe it will eventually become a national park on par with the likes of Gettysburg. The heroes of United Flight 93 deserve America's respect. They must never be forgotten.

Lessons Learned

1. In Every Disaster, There Is Something to Be Grateful For

In a lot of disasters, there is a tendency to immediately find fault, an inclination to blame someone for a lack of preparedness. In the case of the 9-11 terrorist attacks, there was really no one to blame other than the terrorists. As a matter of fact, things could have been much worse.

About fifty thousand people worked in the World Trade Center complex. More than 110,000 visited on a typical business day. That morning, there had been an accident in the Holland Tunnel that prevented many people from getting to work on time. After the planes struck, both towers were quickly evacuated. When the towers fell, most people were already out and far enough away from falling debris. New York firefighters, police, and emergency workers did a great, great job. Hundreds of them gave their lives in the effort.

Every life is precious. 2,824 people innocent people died in the WTC towers on September 11, 2001. But it could have been worse.

More than 24,000 people work in the Pentagon on a normal business day. 125 innocent people died. But it could have been worse.

The four hijacked planes were not full. Some, in fact, were up to three quarters empty. 260 passengers and crew lost their lives on September 11, 2001. That number includes the forty-four people on board United Flight 93 who had time to fight back and save countless lives on the ground. If not for their heroism, it could have been worse.

When you look back on the disaster, there is a lot for which to be grateful.

2. Terrorism Will Never Defeat a Great Nation and Its People

On the day of the attacks, international media outlets broadcast euphoric celebrations in some communities hostile to the United States. Within hours of the strikes, U. S. government intelligence agencies reported that there were "good indications" that the terrorist organization Al Qaeda had planned and carried out the attacks.

Less than a month later, on October 7, 2001, the United States launched an invasion of Afghanistan (where Al Qaeda was based) and removed the Taliban (the country's ruling dictatorship) from power. A videotape and other key information recovered in the war's aftermath proved that U. S. intelligence had been correct.

All across the United States, some great things happened. American patriotism was renewed. Flags were flown from millions of homes in all fifty states. Free citizens vowed not to allow such a thing to ever happen again. And an entire nation rallied around its president, its government, and its military.

On September 11, 2001, international terrorists experienced a temporary, short-lived victory. But in the long run, they did not win. And they will never defeat a great nation and the good people who inhabit it.

Ground zero in early 2005.

Photo by Randall Bell

11

Conclusions

While much of the world is chasing success, I study disasters. I am probably the only person in the world who has worked on and researched all of these sites. I am convinced that they produce unique insights and learning opportunities that are available nowhere else. When disasters happen, they expose the core of individuals, families, governments, leaders, business managers, and organizations. Somehow I always have felt some kind of duty to not only document these experiences, but also to look for some kind of lessons and insights from them.

As an applied economist, disasters have far more dimension than just the dollars and cents. In fact, I don't believe that I could properly do my job without understanding the underlying motivations and behaviors and linking them with their financial effects. I call this a study of "behavioral economics." From such an investigation, we could identify both effective and ineffective traits and management styles. Not only that, but the insights from these real-life conditions certainly would be far more valuable than the anecdotal notions of the pop-success gurus.

Over many years of research, I developed a framework that illustrates, in every case, the issues at the core of both tragedy and triumph. Ultimately, I have discovered that every person and every organization requires four things to be successful; purpose, people, prosperity, and a plan. Our "purpose" is made up of our philosophical and intellectual commitments. "People" consists of our sociological roles and responsibilities, as well as our influences and contacts. Our physical strengths, environment and finances determine our level of "prosperity." Our "plan" consists of developmental goals, daily operations, and the legacy that we ultimately build as a consequence of it all.

Furthermore, I have observed that all behavior falls within one of three categories. "Left line," which is some form of negligence; the "right line," which is the overboard extreme; and the "bottom line" in between. The "bottom line" is where good, effective behavior is found. All behaviors fall within one of these categories. I have tested this paradigm with every crisis that I study, and it always reveals something worthwhile.

Purpose

The starting place for all individuals and organizations lies in defining their "purpose." Philosophically, at Chernobyl we see that the management was "left line" and unprincipled when they ignored the regulations, turned off the safety systems and decided to conduct an unauthorized test. Once the meltdown occurred, the USSR government went again into the "left line" management style of "denial," which only made

		CATEGORIES	MANAGEMENT & BEHAVIORAL STYLE		
		Key Concepts	Left Line™	Bottom Line™	Right Line™
PURPOSE	Philosophical	Our mindset determines the results	Unprincipled	Flexible Principled Passionate	Fanatical
PURPOSE	Intellectual	Intelligence is never above learning	Ignorant	Teachable Knowledgeable Brilliant	Arrogant
PEOPLE	Sociological	Build bridges with friends & barriers for foe	Illicit	Lenient Lawful Considerate	Annoying
PEOPLE	Influential	Family & friends are our best indication of worth	Insensitive	Independent Reliable Supportive	Controlling
PROSPERITY	Physical	Few things matter more than being in good shape	Apathetic	Relaxed Fit Competitive	Excessive
PROSPERITY	Environmental	What surrounds us can become part of us	Careless	Comfortable Orderly Extraordinary	Harsh
PROSPERITY	Financial	One must be solvent to have influence	Insolvent	Generous Budgeted Wealthy	Greedy
PLAN	Developmental	Problem solvers progress	Regressive	Creative Proactive Determined	Irrational
PLAN	Operational	Success comes from putting priorities into action	Negligent	Easy-Going Organized Aggressive	Compulsive
PLAN	Consequential	There are great lessons in both triumphs and tragedies	Denial	Forgiving Accountable Grateful	Obsessive

© Copyright 1991-2005 Bell Consulting.com. All rights reserved. The Bell Matrix. Left Line and Right Line are trademarks of Bell Consulting.

matters worse. We see from Chernobyl that principles of "integrity" and "accountability" are essential.

At the Love Canal, we can observe a group of intellectually well-educated school district board members that went to the other extreme, "right line" arrogance. While they had been directly warned about the dangers in the area, they thought that they knew better than the experts, ignored them and went ahead and built an elementary school smack on top of a toxic waste site. We see from the Love Canal how important being "teachable" really is.

In the O. J. Simpson murder case we can identify all types of behavior. The whole tragedy was caused by O. J.'s "right line" obsessions with Nicole. The prosecution, led by Marcia Clark made many "left line" mistakes and bungled the case. On the other hand, the Brown family operates in the successful "bottom line" by not only supporting each other, but by bringing awareness of domestic abuse into the spotlight through the Nicole Brown Charitable Foundation.

People

Any successful organization must respect society as a whole. In the Marshall Islands, I met with hundreds of people whose lives were deeply affected by our government's decision to go "left line" and detonate the world's largest atomic bomb, while the prevailing winds blew towards inhabited islands.

Monsanto had rules and regulations, but in their "right line" corporate greed, they contaminated vast areas, hurt many people and ultimately paid hundreds of millions of dollars for it. In life and business, we must be considerate of others, build relationships, or pay a hefty price.

Prosperity

All people deserve an opportunity for good health, a safe environment and some measure of financial well-being. Ignoring the left line or right line is at the heart of the billions of dollars of damages that I calculate each year. But the cost of human life is far more. At Mount Saint Helens, the environment was clearly unsafe, yet many people ignored the clear warnings. Today they are buried under hundreds of feet of debris.

Disasters also can show the great side of human nature. During the Great Alaskan Earthquake, Linda McSwain's father held onto his family all night on the roof of their home as the tidal waves battered them. While he probably never expected it, his "bottom line" fitness paid big dividends.

Plan

September 11 showed the horrible effects of "right line" fanaticism, but it also showed the "bottom line" resolve of a great country. Our history shows that, while we may never get over this, we ultimately have gotten through this together. Those with a "problem-solving" mentality ultimately succeed. While everyone is hit with both large and small crises on a nearly continual basis, if we set goals and work our plan, we can get through most anything.

I am often asked by the media which is the world's worst disaster. My answer is always the same, "Auschwitz." Simply stated, this is the most awful display of "right line" fanaticism and human behavior imaginable. Many people would like to simply not think about it. Yet, as I visited the death camps, I admired those who went to great efforts to insure that the world preserves the legacy of these difficult but valuable lessons. There are great lessons in both triumphs and tragedies.

Most behavioral models crumble under the pressure of the kinds of situations that I deal with. On the other hand, this framework stands up to every challenge from the most extreme of conditions. With every circumstance, this model can be used to better understand the behaviors involved, what worked, what didn't and can allow one to take away important lessons. While the left line, right line and bottom line concepts may appear to be simple and self-evident, they are frequently ignored. Indeed, crossing over into either the right line or left line areas results in more than $40 billion in damage per year, just in the category of real estate alone. The loss to business and lives makes this figure much higher.

From my consulting work and research of the world's great disasters, I am convinced that as both individuals and organizations avoid both the "left line" and "right line" extremes, strive for balance, and make a contentious effort to navigate only within the "bottom line" areas, more and more problems will be avoided. This means that those who conscientiously stay within this zone will inevitably enjoy good "bottom line" results and a higher level of achievement.

About the Authors

Randall Bell is the CEO of Bell Anderson & Sanders LLC, a consulting firm that specializes in business and real estate damage economics. Randy works in the areas of strategic planning, problem solving and crisis management, as well determining the financial impacts of detrimental conditions.

Throughout his career, Randy has consulted in many high-profile cases ranging from terrorist attacks (the World Trade Center site, United Flight 93 crash site), crime scenes (OJ Simpson, Jon Benet Ramsey), mass-suicide (Heaven's Gate), nuclear test sites (the Bikini Atoll in the Marshall Islands), pipeline explosions (Durham Woods), landslides (Laguna Niguel), as well as riots, floods, earthquakes, and environmental damage. His clients include federal, state and municipal governments, major corporations, real estate developers, and insurance companies.

A frequent speaker at events worldwide, Randy has appeared on *Court TV*, *Entertainment Tonight*, the *O'Reilly Factor*, CNN, *Extra* and every major television network. His career has been profiled in the *San Francisco Chronicle*, the *New York Times*, the *Chicago Tribune*, the *Los Angeles Times*, *The Wall Street Journal,* and *People Magazine*, as well as the international media.

Randy is the author of the textbook, *Real Estate Damages,* which is published by the Appraisal Institute, and his valuation methodologies have been incorporated into federal guidelines. He sits on the Board of Directors of the *Nicole Brown Foundation* and the Advisory Board of the *Bureau of National Affairs* in Washington DC.

The author of several other books, Randy wrote the Owners Manual quick-reference series, which includes the *Home Owners Manual* and the *Business Owners Manual*. He has a BS degree from BYU and an MBA degree from UCLA. Randy resides in Southern California with his wife and four children.

About the Authors

A best-selling author of major works of nonfiction, **Don Phillips** is known for his ability to tell stories and bring history alive with crisp compelling prose. His trilogy on American leadership (*The Founding Fathers on Leadership*, *Lincoln on Leadership*, *Martin Luther King, Jr. on Leadership*) has won worldwide acclaim. His first book, *Lincoln on Leadership*, paved the way toward the creation of an entire new genre of books on historical leadership.

Books by Donald T. Phillips

Lincoln on Leadership (Warner Books; 1992)

On The Brink: The Life and Leadership of Norman Brinker (with Norman Brinker; Summit; 1996)

Lincoln Stories for Leaders (Summit, 1997)

The Founding Fathers on Leadership (Warner Books; 1997)

Martin Luther King, Jr. on Leadership (Warner Books; 1999)

A Diamond in Spring (Summit; 1999)

Leading with the Heart: Coach K's Successful Strategies in Basketball, Business, and Life (by Mike Krzyzewski; Warner Books; 2000)

Run To Win: Vince Lombardi on Coaching and Leadership (St. Martin's Press; 2001)

Five Point Play: The Story of Duke's Amazing 2000-2001 Championship Season (by Mike Krzyzewski; Warner Books, 2001)

Unto Us a Child: Abuse and Deception in the Catholic Church (Tapestry Books; 2002)

Character in Action: The U.S. Coast Guard on Leadership (with Admiral James M. Loy; Naval Institute Press; 2003)

The Rudy in You: A Youth Sports Guide for Players, Parents, and Coaches (with Rudy Ruettiger and Peter Leddy; Bonus Books, 2005)

One Magical Sunday (But Winning Isn't Everything) (by Phil Mickelson; Warner Books, 2005)